THE POPULAR GUIDE
TO THE MASS

THE
POPULAR
GUIDE
TO THE
MASS

William Marrevee, S.C.J.

The Pastoral Press
Washington, DC 20011

ISBN: 0-912405-93-7

The Pastoral Press
225 Sheridan Street, NW
Washington, DC 20011
(202) 723-1254

The Pastoral Press is the Publications Division of the National Associaton of Pastoral Musicians, a membership organization of musicians and clergy dedicated to fostering the art of musical liturgy.

Printed in the United States of America.

Contents

Introduction

When we prepare children for "their first communion" in the parish where I am privileged to minister, we like to insist that the primary purpose of this preparation is to stimulate our children to acquire a liking, a taste, or an affinity for what we, the Christian community, love to do on Sunday mornings. The emphasis is not on *their* "first," but on what *we do* as a eucharistic community. This is not unique to our parish. An increasing number of parishes are following this approach and for very good reasons. The best way to prepare our children is to offer them authentic celebrations of the eucharist in their parish. The emphasis is less on the frantic search for the latest in "first communion preparation programs," and more on having our parishioners reflect on what we do on Sunday morning. If that is understood, it will not be hard to find ways to help our children discover and cultivate a taste for the eucharistic expression of their faith life. It will also have the fringe benefit of eliminating the need for special "first communion celebrations" which reduce the rest of the parish community to interested spectators. In addition it will make parishes take their Sunday eucharist more seriously.

The theological reflections on the eucharist presented in this book are the result, on the one hand, of having had the privilege of teaching the course on the eucharist at Saint Paul University and at a number of other academic institutions for a few years and, on the other hand, of having worked with groups of parents, teachers, priests, and pastoral workers in the context of meetings, workshops, and short courses sponsored by a considerable number of parishes, dioceses, school boards, and religious communities. When I have been invited to speak on the eucharist in these different settings I have tried to prod the participants into a reflection on *what* it is that they are doing when they assemble to celebrate the eucharist. This is not to suggest that the question of *how* we go about doing eucharist is not important. But I believe that the *how* will be pretty well taken care of when we have a profound appreciation of *what* it is that we are doing.

That is the aim of these theological reflections on the eucharist. They stay very close to the basic outline and constituent parts of the liturgical rite of the eucharist itself. The reason for this option will be explained in the book. Other approaches to the eucharist are possible but the approach presented here has been tested in practice and has received a favorable hearing not only from theology students but also from those who love to assemble as a church on the Day of the Lord week-in-and-week-out. Consequently, these reflections are presented in the hope that they will enrich the readers' understanding of the eucharist and, better still, their love for it.

My sincere thanks go to those who have heard me speak about the eucharist in various contexts and have helped me, by their questions, criticisms, and observations, to clarify many points. I am greatly indebted to Murielle Neville who spent many hours transcribing a number of my recorded talks so that I might use them as the basis for this manuscript. Many thanks as well to Dr. Kenneth Russell who painstakingly and ruthlessly went through the text to make the English more presentable. Finally, a special word of gratitude to the members of St. Mark's parish community with whom it has been a delight to celebrate the eucharist for the last thirteen years.

CHAPTER ONE

Some Convictions and Some Handicaps

Our involvement in a ritual activity such as the eucharist is very much conditioned by the fact that we participate as Christians. Do we really have to mention this? The point is that, from a purely human perspective, we could see ourselves doing much of what we do at eucharist for a variety of reasons and for other than strictly eucharistic purposes. The experience of assembling at a given place and of seeing one of the assembled take a presiding role is not uncommon. The same applies to the two central activities that constitute the community's eucharistic activity: having a few passages from a collection of books read to us and sharing bread and wine, while some words are being spoken and some acclamations and songs are being sung. In other words, the immediately observable things we do at eucharist are not unusual. It is the sort of ritual to which, with varying degrees of solemnity, we have recourse when we want to mark a wide range of occasions, from the visit of a head of state to the wedding of our daughter to the birthday of a special friend.

When we engage in these simple activities "in memory of Jesus," the very meaning of these activities is shaped and colored by who this Jesus is and how we as individual men and women and as an assembled community relate to him. In other words,

3

there are some basic Christian convictions being expressed in these activities. We bring these convictions with us when we do the activities "in memory of Jesus." The result is that the otherwise quite ordinary activities we engage in take on a new meaning. In fact, the convictions establish the real meaning of the activities without destroying or simply by-passing their original meaning.

At the same time, we must be conscious of the fact that, for almost two thousand years now, many generations of Christians have engaged in these activities in the most diverse situations imaginable. Yes, the basic activities may have remained virtually the same, but it should cause no surprise to see that the actual circumstances in which the eucharist has been celebrated have profoundly affected it. They have all left their mark. Imagine the difference between a eucharist celebrated by Christians enduring persecution and a eucharist celebrated by Christians whose faith is the official religion of the state. The socio-political circumstances condition the celebration of the eucharist.

But in addition to these socio-political factors, there are also important theological factors that, in the course of the church's history, have left their mark on the way the eucharist was and still is perceived. What comes to mind are the theological reflections and controversies in the ninth and eleventh centuries and the tragic controversies with the Reformation Churches since the sixteenth century. The resulting theological polemics have had their effect on the eucharist and still condition us today. Though the average participant in the eucharist today may have no idea of what particular points were made in those periods, the eucharist that he or she participates in and the manner in which he or she participates in it is very much affected by them. These various socio-political and theological factors have led to the development of some unique emphases and possibly even some blind spots both in our eucharistic practice and in our understanding of the eucharist.

I have chosen to deal with these convictions and handicaps first in the hope that facing up to them will facilitate the reading of the rest of the book. I spell out the convictions in an attempt to es-tablish the wavelength I would like to use to approach the eucharist. It is a matter of "putting my cards on the table". I do hope that these convictions are not so subjective that the readers cannot share them. I readily admit, however, that they could be phrased quite differently. The point is that we bring certain convictions to our celebration of the eucharist. Little is gained from leaving these unmentioned or from simply presupposing them and leaving them unarticulated.

As for spelling out the handicaps, that is a slightly different matter. There are several sets of handicaps that need our attention if we are to be realistic about the conditions under which our communities celebrate the eucharist today. Only recently, M. Francis Mannion has outlined the basic features of a cultural mood that is not very well disposed to honoring the Day of the Lord by way of celebrating the eucharist.[1] The characteristics which Mannion detects may be more immediately applicable to the contemporary scene in the United States, but many of them find an echo in what marks the cultural climate in the Canadian context as well. Familiarity with and attentiveness to these contemporary cultural characteristics will show why the combination of Sunday and eucharist is not as self-evident any more as it once was.

The handicaps which I would like to draw attention to are of a more theological kind. Some may consider that I have been a bit biased in this section. On the other hand, it is not too difficult to see that, in the course of the church's history, some important shifts have occurred and that some aspects of the eucharist have received so much emphasis that our understanding of it as an integral whole has suffered. These shifts of emphasis still play tricks on us and cloud our vision. They function as obstacles that absorb a disproportionate amount of time and energy at the expense of other, perhaps even more basic, aspects of the eucharist. This is especially true when we consider how much the eucharist has changed in a relatively short period of time. Moving from the priest's Mass to the community's celebration of the eucharist is not a smooth transition.

Some Basic Christian Convictions

1. The eucharist is not some isolated incident. It does not stand on its own. The true meaning of the eucharist comes to light only

in relation to the Jesus Christ event which is made present in it. That is to say, the Jesus Christ event itself, more particularly the paschal mystery of Christ, is the real explanation of what the eucharist is. But this Jesus Christ event is not an isolated event either. On the contrary, in the life, death, and resurrection of Jesus a gracious God has initiated a transformation, a liberation, a whole (holy)-making of us. In Jesus, God has bonded himself to us and us to himself and each of us to one another in a new and unheard of way. In other words, the Jesus Christ event and the eucharist must be situated in the history of God's grace-filled dealings with humanity. This history has not yet reached its intended goal. Nevertheless, God's relationship with us and our relationship with God is shaped in a unique way in and through the paschal mystery of Christ. When the eucharist makes this paschal mystery of Christ present among us in a sacramental or in a ritual-symbolic way, we have a perfect example of what all Christian liturgy basically is: the acting out or articulation in a ritual-symbolic fashion of how it is between God and us on account of Jesus Christ. The way in which this relationship is acted out allows it to take hold of us ever more firmly and to define our Christian identity ever anew. When we as a Christian community engage in eucharistic activity, we do not simply acknowledge the existence of some faceless, anonymous Supreme Being; we communicate with the God and Father of Jesus Christ whom we are privileged to call our Father because the Spirit dwells in us.

2. The eucharist is all about the life-project of Jesus: the Kingdom of God. Jesus lived for this and laid down his life for it. But the life story of Jesus does not stop there. We Christians profess this Jesus to be Lord. We believe that the God to whom he bore faithful witness raised him from the dead and thus established him as the cornerstone of God's Kingdom and first-born of a new humanity. That living, dying, and being raised from the dead is made present among us in the eucharist in the power of the Spirit. This is the significance of keeping the memorial of Jesus Christ which characterizes the celebration of the eucharist. We do not keep memorial of Jesus Christ as spectators nor do we look upon his living, dying, and being raised from the dead as some past event. As his disciples we dare, in the power of the Spirit, to enter into his living,

6

dying, and being raised from the dead so as to be empowered to make a contribution in our time to the ongoing realization of the life-project of Jesus, the completion of which still awaits us and lies beyond this history.

3. When we engage in eucharistic activity we come as men and women who live in a given place and in a particular time. That is to say, we come together with all our hopes and our fears, our pain and joy, with all the stuff that makes up our life-stories; we come marked by the exciting and frightening features of our world. But we come together because of the light that a gracious God has shed on our existence in Jesus Christ. We come together because we believe that in the Jesus Christ event our individual and communal life stories have been placed against a new horizon, God's horizon. And our wager is that the more we let our life stories and our world be submerged in this Jesus Christ event, the more we will find ourselves on a path that leads to life. So we keep coming back to that Jesus Christ event, because as Christians we argue that there is nowhere else to go, if we want to make sense of life. With our life stories grafted onto the life story of Jesus Christ we trust that we are not on a dead-end street; on the contrary, we are confident that we are on a path that leads to life and light. All this is contained in the faith conviction that in the life, death, and resurrection of Jesus something concerning our lives has come to light that we no longer can or want to do without. We are prepared to acknowledge and celebrate in praise and thanksgiving that in Jesus Christ a gracious God has introduced a new dynamic into human history and we let ourselves be caught up in that dynamic. Here we celebrate God, not just any kind of God, but a God we have come to know in Jesus, a God who wants to be our God.

4. When it comes to celebrating eucharist, we adhere to a basic ritual with a simple outline. It has its own flow and its own laws which must be respected. Certainly, the basic script can be executed with greater or lesser solemnity, some modifications can be introduced, but the ritual is given to us and we act within its basic outline. Yet, important as the ritual is, the eucharist has more to do with our basic stance in life than with the performance of a given ritual. The authenticity of the eucharist is not safeguarded by the proper execution of its ritual. The issue of authenticity or

whether we are dealing with a true eucharist is decided neither by the sort of bread we use nor by the alcohol content of the wine, but by the quality of life of the community that celebrates the eucharist. What sort of vision, what sort of commitment to God's kingdom of justice and peace here and now in this world do we bring to the eucharist or do we hope to see nourished by it?

5. The following point is not so much a basic Christian conviction as a basic presupposition that underlies my understanding of the eucharist. Even though the presiding minister has an important place in its celebration, it is nevertheless the community of baptized-confirmed men and women that celebrates the eucharist. To be more explicit, it is not the priest who celebrates the eucharist for the community, but the community that celebrates the eucharist which is presided over by one of its members who has been mandated, by ordination, for the ministry of presiding over the eucharistic community. This makes the presider into a real eucharistic minister, but he—in the Roman Catholic tradition we still have to use the masculine pronoun to designate this particular eucharistic minister—is not the only eucharistic minister. For the assembled community to celebrate the eucharist adequately, various ministries are needed:

- ministry of hospitality
- ministry of presiding
- ministry of reading the word of God
- ministry of preaching
- ministry of distributing the eucharist
- ministry of leading the community's singing
- ministry of assisting the presider (to be preferred over altar boys or girls or servers).

All these ministries have to be understood as ministries to the community of baptized-confirmed men and women that has assembled to celebrate the eucharist. This is what makes them eucharistic ministries. Those who minister are not there to help the priest, but the community. Only one of them is there to assist the presiding minister; all the others, including the priest, are there to assist the eucharistic community. The fact that we are baptized-confirmed Christians empowers us to provide these ministries to the eucharistic community, with the exception of the ministry of presiding and normally that of preaching. In these cases, in addition to being baptized-confirmed, a person needs to be ordained.

Some Handicaps from the Past

In order to keep this section from appearing entirely negative, the points to be made here must be seen against the larger background of what previous generations have succeeded in handing on to us, namely the eucharist. We are greatly indebted to them for the immense treasure we have received. But such indebtedness cannot blind us to some of the flaws of the eucharist as it has come down to us. These flaws, of course, do not affect the core of the eucharist, but they may keep it from standing out with as much clarity as it could.

This century's liturgical renewal has clearly exposed these flaws but they still sometimes impede the consistent implementation of liturgical reform. I expose them here simply to identify certain problem areas that we will inevitably encounter when we try to proceed with the ongoing eucharistic reform. I hope that the rest of the book will set the issues raised here in a different context. It may even become apparent later on that some of the issues that have been so tragically controversial lose their sharp edges and contentious features when they are placed in a different context. One could argue that the best way to proceed is to forget about trying to dialogue with previously held positions and to make a straightforward presentation of what the eucharist means in its present form. The point, however, is that these previously held positions still appeal to many people who find it difficult to reconcile them with a more contemporary, more biblically and patristically based understanding of the eucharist. "Was the previous understanding not biblical and patristic?" some could ask. And here we will have to say that indeed it often lacked a biblical and patristic depth, and that this was precisely the principal reason why the eucharist became the prisoner of tragic controversies.

The points raised here presuppose a certain degree of familiarity with the history of eucharistic practice and thought. If we want to understand the present concerns or difficulties, we shall have to appeal to history on occasion. And history will prove to be a good teacher because it will make us understand the present better. We must be willing to ask whether there are factors in that history which can explain why we find it hard to consistently implement eucharistic reform. Does this focus lead to a selective or even biased reading of history? It does not necessarily have to lead to that, although it must be admitted that there is always a certain amount of interpretation in this way of reading history. We must be careful that we do not end up with a distorted reading.

1. It is not that long ago that the standard Roman Catholic reply to the question "What are the parts of the Mass?" was: "offertory, consecration, communion". We shall have to say something more about this very unfortunate, if not in fact faulty designation of some parts of the Mass. What is really striking in this designation is that not a word is said about the liturgy of the word. For centuries, in the Roman Catholic tradition, the liturgy of the word was simply not considered to be an important, let alone a constitutive part of the eucharist. The result has been quite tragic.

In the sixteenth century, the Reformers pointed out the built-in dangers of neglecting the liturgy of the word and of placing all the emphasis on what happens around the bread and wine. Their critique was not welcomed, and the polemics that followed did not make the situation much better. In some ways, it made matters even worse. The Reformation Churches tended to emphasize the word so much that, in many instances, they played down the importance of the rest of the eucharist. Hence the infrequent celebration of the eucharist in many of these churches. On the Roman Catholic side, it was felt necessary to defend and emphasize what the Reformers neglected. As is often the case, the undue attention to one part without a matching respect for the other actually impoverishes the part that is being emphasized. In the context of the eucharist, the word cannot do without the sacrament proper, nor can the sacrament proper do without the word. There has to be a healthy interaction between both word and sacrament, otherwise both suffer.

What a welcome change, then, to have the General Instruction of the Roman Missal state unambiguously: "The Mass is made up as it were of the liturgy of the word and the liturgy of the eucharist, two parts so closely connected that they form but one single act of worship."[2] Significant progress has been made in giving the liturgy of the word its due place within the celebration of the eucharist, but there are also indications that, because of the long centuries of neglect, we are not yet totally at ease with accepting the liturgy of the word as an inherent part of the eucharist. As a result, people expect different things from the liturgy of the word and therefore, at times, it is used for purposes that are actually extrinsic to the community's celebration of the eucharist.

2. It may be somewhat risky to speak of the "Real Presence" issue as a handicap towards a more integral understanding of the church's eucharist, but that is the truth of the matter. There has been, first of all, an unwarranted concentration on the real presence of Christ in the consecrated bread and wine. I am not suggesting we deny the real presence of Christ in the elements. How could one deny such an important aspect of eucharistic faith! The problem is that this one mode of Christ's presence has been singled out to the neglect of the three other modes in which the risen Christ is really present in the community's celebration of the eucharist: in the assembled community, in the presiding minister, and in the word proclaimed. Number 7 of the Constitution on the Sacred Liturgy is quite explicit about affirming the fourfold presence of Christ in the eucharist.[3] It is a major task to show how these four modes of Christ's presence, precisely in their interaction with and their dependence on each other, constitute the eucharist, but this can only be done when we stop speaking of Christ's real presence almost exclusively in relation to the consecrated bread and wine.

The second point in reference to this almost exclusive interest in the consecrated bread concerns the shift of focus that, in the course of history, has taken place in the dominant eucharistic symbols. It is a shift that Nathan Mitchell, among others, has documented well.[4] The eucharistic symbols that were originally dominant were actions: assembling, proclaiming-listening, thanking, sharing bread and wine. But, in great part because of the eucharistic controversies of the ninth and eleven centuries, the elements of bread and wine became the dominant symbols. The interest was no longer

11

action-oriented but object-oriented. This is especially true of the consecrated bread which came to be known as the blessed sacrament. It is no longer the entire eucharistic action which is identified as the sacrament but the consecrated bread and wine as objects.

This shift from action to object has had enormous eucharistic and ecclesiological implications. The more immediately evident eucharistic implications are the various eucharistic devotions which have become a hallmark of Roman Catholic piety: adoration of the blessed sacrament, processions with the blessed sacrament, and visits to the blessed sacrament that sprang up from an almost isolated handling of the eucharistic bread. Because of this concentration on the consecrated bread it also became possible to receive communion apart from the eucharistic action itself. Receiving communion was considered more of a devotional exercise than an integral part of the community's celebration of the eucharist. An additional feature of this development was the prominent place assigned to the tabernacle in our churches. This affected our perception of the nature of the church building. Instead of it being the place where the Christian community assembles as the Body of Christ, the church building became the place where the blessed sacrament is kept.

No doubt, many aspects of these eucharistic devotions are legitimate, but if they become so prominent that they obscure and in some instances even hinder the primary thrust of the church's eucharist, then we should be very cautious.

3. An even touchier issue involves "the sacrifice of the Mass." It has been the most contentious issue in our relations with the Reformation Churches. It has also become a controversial issue in Roman Catholic circles as a result of the recent eucharistic reform which prompts people to ask: "Is the Mass a sacrifice or is it a meal?" But when we apply the notions of sacrifice and meal to the eucharist, are the terms mutually exclusive?

What makes the issue of the "sacrifice of the Mass" so very difficult to handle are the many unarticulated assumptions about sacrifice and the occasional carelessness with which this delicate category is used. We have to realize that there may be a fair distance between theological reflection on this issue and the more popular perception of it displayed in the way the Mass is actually used. Theology, which admits that images other than those associated with sacrifice also capture the significance of the eucharist, uses considerable finesse to demonstrate the legitimacy of using this term in relation to the eucharist. It is a different matter when we consider what the term evokes on the more popular level. What function do people think the sacrifice of the Mass plays in our relationship with God? Is it simply a concretization of a sacrificial system that fits into some general notion of religion? But in that case is the uniqueness of the Jesus Christ event, which shapes our relationship with God so that it is clear that it is based on God's reaching out to us in mercy and grace rather than on anything we offer to God, sufficiently respected? If speaking of the sacrifice of the Mass is legitimate because the death of Christ is made present in the Mass in a sacramental way, where does this leave the rest of the life story of Jesus and his life project, namely the Kingdom of God? Where does this almost exclusive preoccupation with his death leave his being raised from the dead? What is the significance of the sacrifice of the Mass being linked so intimately with an imposing crucifix hanging over the altar of sacrifice?

Questions of this sort cannot be brushed aside as merely speculative or as too intricate, when we consider that, precisely on the popular level, the Mass is seen as a sacrifice that can be offered for a great variety of needs and especially for the dead. Does this use of the Mass not reflect an unacceptable narrowing of what the church's eucharist is all about?

4. Another element connected with the prominence of the sacrifie of the Mass is the significant impact it has had on the notion of priesthood. The sacrifice of the Mass and priesthood are very much correlative terms. The increasing prominence of the sacrifice of the Mass has also pushed the notion of priesthood in a sacrificial direction. This in turn must be seen as the inevitable outcome of the increasingly prominent role of the priest and the correspondingly decreasing role of the community in the eucharist. It can best be illustrated by some popular expressions: "The priest says the Mass or offers the sacrifice of the Mass and the faithful attend or

have the priest offer a Mass for a variety of purposes." The Mass becomes so much the property of the priest that he can say Mass all by himself without the presence of the community. This is a far cry from the community of baptized-confirmed men and women celebrating the eucharist presided over by an ordained minister.

5. There have been some regrettable developments within the eucharistic celebration itself. Perhaps the most glaring of all is the alarming absence of a true appreciation of the integrity of the eucharistic prayer and of its unique place in the eucharist. Not only did this presidential prayer become identified as the priest's prayer but one of its sections was so disastrously blown out of proportion that it was no longer recognized as part of the entire eucharistic prayer which has a coherence of its own. This coherence is seriously distorted when one of its parts is allowed to overshadow every other part. I am referring, of course, to the virtually exclusive interest in the institution narrative narrowly interpreted as the words of consecration. The losses the eucharist has suffered on account of this are beyond imagining. The eucharistic prayer is certainly not the entire eucharist, but it does occupy such a central place that if its true nature is no longer understood and if, as a consequence, one section of it, namely the institution narrative, is so emphasized that it eclipses the rest of the prayer the disorientation is quite evident. Therefore, the recovery of the sense that the entire eucharistic prayer is the church's eminent profession of faith and the realization of how the institution narrative functions within it to authorize the community to celebrate the eucharist will go a long way toward helping us achieve a more integral understanding of the eucharist.

When we look back at the handicaps that have hindered the development of an understanding and practice of the eucharist consonant with the intended eucharistic reform, we detect a certain pattern. Very often what happens is that legitimate aspects of the eucharist are emphasized to such an extent that they begin to lead an almost independent existence. Once they are taken out of their proper context, they draw so much attention to themselves that we have difficulty discerning how they are supposed to function within the larger context of the community's celebration of the eucharist. Much of our work will consist in reintegrating these various aspects in their proper context in the hope that we may arrive at what I would like to call a more integral and coherent understanding of the eucharist.

* * * * * *

Now that we have spelled out these convictions and handicaps, we are in a position to try to put forward some theological reflections on the eucharist that stay close to its liturgical rite. This attempt is made on the premise that a significant theology of the eucharist can be constructed on the basis of the way the church does eucharist.

Notes

1. M. Francis Mannion, "Sunday in Modern America: A Cultural Perspective," *Chicago Studies* (1990) 224-235.

2. General Instruction of the Roman Missal no. 8.

3. Ibid. no. 7.

4. Nathan Mitchell, *Cult and Controversy: The Worship of the Eucharist Outside Mass* (New York: Pueblo Publishing Co., 1982) 3-198.

CHAPTER TWO

The Four Elements
of the Eucharist

When speaking of "elements" in the context of the eucharist, we have become accustomed to think immediately of bread and wine. Of course, bread and wine are important for eucharist. However, for a true appreciation of what makes eucharist we must not be too object-oriented because, after all, the dominant eucharistic symbols are actions. Opting for a broader conception of the "elements" of the eucharist has important ramifications.

If a reporter, with no particular interest in the faith reality the community is involved in, were to write up a report on what she sees us doing on Sunday morning, she might be expected to make the following observations. Leaving aside particular details, she would see a good number of men and women come together in one given place. It would be hard to detect a common feature among them in terms of social class or age group, except, unfortunately, for the fact that the very poor and teen-agers are often under-represented. But otherwise, it is an interesting mix of people of different ages, from the very young to the very old, of different social status, and different ethnic backgrounds. They come as families, as couples, as single people, as a small cluster of friends. Once they have all taken their place, they seem to adhere to a script with which, with a few exceptions, they are all fairly familiar. Part of the script is that at least one of them is dressed quite differently from the rest and takes a leading role. He does not, however, monopolize the action and leave the rest of the people gathered together no option but to play the role of passive spectators. On the contrary, while he maintains a position of prominence throughout the ceremony, a good number of activities are performed by other members of the group. These activities seem to be arranged to facilitate the exercise of the participants' right of ownership over the corporate activity for which they have come together. The reporter would get the impression that it is not some amorphous group that happens to be together in one place for a while and then disperses again. It is a well structured group of people that form a community that seems to be involved in something that is quite important to it. The participants are engaged in a corporate activity that runs quite smoothly and that holds few, if any, surprises.

The hour-long group activity is fairly well orchestrated. The group physically alternates between standing, sitting, and kneeling. There is some singing; words that seem to follow familiar formulas are interchanged between the presider and the rest of the group. At one point the presider speaks at some length to the group, but quite often, on their behalf, he addresses a reality that is not visible to the human eye. All seem to be quite conscious of this invisible presence or at least to be in communication with it. In whatever way these people interact with this unseen reality which they call God, their group activity gravitates around two focal points. The one is marked by the reading of a few passages from a book that has pride of place in the first part of their corporate activity. They call it the Bible or the Scriptures. All listen attentively to these readings and when the presider addresses the participants at some length, he seems to be taking his cue from what has been read from that book. Once that is dealt with, then the focus shifts to the second rallying point. Bread and wine are placed on what could be described as a table and the presider, without losing contact with the group, proceeds to speak to the reality that they identify as God. Notions of thanksgiving and interceding are particularly prominent in this speaking, but whatever the presider says to God does not seem to be improvised on the spot. It follows a set pattern and has a content that all present seem to be familiar with, because every so often they make their own voice heard through short responses or acclamations which are usually sung. All this is done over bread and wine which the presider lifts up at the end of his speaking to God. Shortly after, he breaks the bread and almost everyone present comes forward to share some bread and wine. The group stays together for a few closing gestures, activities, or words, but not long after they have received the bread and wine, the members of the group disperse.

This may be a rather simplistic way of describing the eucharist. It may have the advantage, though, of showing how elementary it is. Seeing people congregate, having one of them preside, listening to some readings, and sharing bread and wine are the basic elements of our eucharistic activity. Taking these ordinary gestures together we have here the basic outline of what eucharist is, at least from a non-believing observer's perspective. But, in addition to these four elements which anyone can observe, there is a fifth which is so decisively different that it is better to consider it a quality which pervades the four elements and places them in the realm of faith. With this God-given quality we read and interpret the gestures and activities described above from a faith perspective, and we see that something more than meets the eye takes place here. It is this something more that preoccupies us. We shall not, however, skip over the elementary activities that we have briefly outlined. We want to give them their due, but we also want to pay attention to what we are able to affirm about them in faith. After all, from a faith perspective, we hold that these very ordinary activities are the bearers of something that touches on the very identity of this group of men and women, especially in their relationship with God and with each other.

What is at issue here and what constitutes the real significance of the four elements taken together and read in the light of faith is the point that number 7 of the Constitution on the Sacred Liturgy makes when it speaks of the fourfold presence of Christ in the church's celebration of the eucharist. It states that the risen Christ is present in the community that has assembled in his name, in the presiding minister, in the proclamation of the word and in the bread and wine over which the prayer of praise and thanksgiving is being proclaimed and that are subsequently consumed. This statement of the constitution which points out that all of the church's liturgy is really Christ's work, and it is the church's work only to the extent that Christ, in the power of the Spirit, is at work in the church or that we are united with Christ, applies to the entire range of the Church's liturgy. Only then can the church's liturgy worship God and sanctify people. But the significance of the constitution's statement comes to light particularly when we apply it to the eucharist, for in that context it enables us to arrive at a faith interpretation of the elements described above.

The four modes of Christ's presence referred to here are not isolated ways in which the risen Christ is present. No, it is precisely in their reciprocal interaction that they make the very ordinary human actions of assembling, of presiding, of proclaiming, of saying thanksgiving over and sharing bread and wine into the church's eucharist. In this case it is important for the integrity of the church's eucharist that we refrain from attributing the notion of real presence almost exclusively to the consecrated bread and wine. Not only does this object-oriented outlook easily lead to a rather static perception of Christ's presence in the bread and wine, but it also tends to devalue the other three modes in which Christ is really present in the power of the Spirit in the church's eucharist. So this insistence on the fourfold presence of Christ has much to do, on the one hand, with recapturing the significance of Christ's active and real presence in the community, in the presiding minister, in the word proclaimed and, on the other hand, with relativizing or at least contextualizing Christ's active and real presence in the bread and wine over which the prayer of thanksgiving is proclaimed. Christ's presence in the bread and wine only makes sense in interaction with the other three modes of Christ's real presence. If it is totally isolated from the other three, it becomes extremely difficult to handle correctly. In fact, it is only when we accept and respect the full import of this fourfold presence of Christ that we can find an adequate explanation of why, from a faith perspective, Christians can make the claim that the four ordinary elements are transformed into the church's eucharist.

We are now in a position to identify the four elements that make up the community's celebration of the eucharist:

1. We come together, we assemble in one place as a community of baptized-confirmed men and women;

2. One of us presides over this assembling on the basis of being mandated, by ordination, for this service to the community;

3. We listen to the proclamation of God's word;

4. We praise and thank God over bread and wine which we subsequently eat and drink.

The four modes of Christ's presence provide us with the basic outline of the eucharist. They correspond perfectly with the four elements that make up the church's eucharist. We will briefly comment on the first two elements in the rest of this chapter. The remainder of the book will be devoted to the last two elements in order to demonstrate how the assembled community presided over by the ordained minister does eucharist when it listens to the Scriptures and gives praise and thanks to God over bread and wine which are then shared.

We Assemble as the Church

The first element of the eucharist is a group of people coming together or assembling in one place as a community of baptized-confirmed men and women. Since this is one of those actions we so easily take for granted, its profound significance may escape us. It would be unfortunate if we continued to pay scant attention to it, because a faith-reflection on this coming together in one place, which seems so ordinary and so functional, can bring to light aspects of the eucharist that we must grasp if we are to make sense of what we as a community are about to do. A proper appreciation of what this assembling means will also enhance our appreciation of the eucharist, because this assembling is already part of it. The Orthodox theologian Alexander Schmemann has some insightful reflections on this aspect of the church's eucharist in his book *The Eucharist. Sacrament of the Kingdom*. Although I am tempted to simply quote the entire chapter entitled "The Sacrament of the Assembly,"[1] because you will find few, if any, places where the eucharistic significance of the simple action of assembling is taken so seriously, I shall confine myself to highlighting a few points.

These are baptized-confirmed men and women that assemble. However different they may be in every other respect, there is one factor that underlies their coming together in this place, at this hour, on this day. It is their being grafted onto Jesus Christ by means of a faith sealed in the sacraments of initiation that made them, in Johannine terms, be born of God or, in Pauline terms, enter into the death and resurrection of Christ. Made one with and in Jesus Christ and filled with the Holy Spirit, they have become the sons and daughters of God and, as such, members of the Body of Christ, the church. The coming together of these men and women in one given place is the visible manifestation and concrete realization of their being the Body of Christ, the church. Here we come together as the church. As Roman Catholics, we are inclined to think and speak of church more immediately in universal terms. That is due to the so-called universalist ecclesiology which is so dominant in our church. What we need to recover is the church-quality, the ecclesialness of the local assembly. This is not to suggest that one ecclesiology be played against the other. That would be counterproductive. It is more a matter of retrieving the sense that in this local assembly the Body of Christ, the church, is concretely being realized.

In these men and women assembled for eucharist we stumble upon the new people of God. Our assembling manifests the unity that God dreams about for the entire human family and for which he has laid the cornerstone in the death and resurrection of Jesus Christ, the New Adam. This unity, anchored in Jesus Christ, is far from complete and, therefore, these men and women need to assemble as the Body of Christ to concretely manifest what they already are in part and to become what they are not yet fully. Our act of assembling reveals what we are already, namely the Body of Christ, but we assemble in the hope that what we are already may become fuller by means of the celebration of the eucharist. Part of this is that by assembling we give visible expression to our having become brothers and sisters in Jesus Christ. We may be spouses, parents and children, neighbors and friends or strangers to each other on the human level, but, because we have been baptized-confirmed, we are brothers and sisters, we are the Body of Christ of which the celebration of the eucharist is the sacrament. That is, then, what our assembling for eucharist embodies. It has a great deal to do with the intimate unity which binds the assembly, the eucharist, and the church together.

Schmemann, therefore, speaks of the assembly as the primary form of the eucharist. The assembly is the first and basic act of the eucharist. The eucharistic liturgy does not begin after the people are in their places: the gathering itself is the first liturgical act of the eucharist, its foundation and beginning. This sheds some light on the common expression: we are going to church. At first sight, we understand this to mean that we are going to a particular building. But as Schmemann points out:

> When I say that I am going to church, it means I am going into the assembly of the faithful in order, together with them, to constitute the Church, in order to be what I became on the day of my baptism—a member, in the fullest, absolute meaning of the term, of the body of Christ. "You are the body of Christ and individually members of it", says the apostle (I Cor. 12:27). I go to manifest and realize my membership, to manifest and witness before God and the world the mystery of the Kingdom of God, which already "has come in power".[2]

The church building that we go to is the site where the real church gathers.

It may very well be that one of the reasons why so many stay away from church on Sunday is that they lack the sense of constituting the Body of Christ in this place. There seems to be little awareness of what it means to be members of the Body of Christ. Many people may vaguely subscribe to the notion, but seem to have no idea that this has concrete implications in terms of giving visible expression to it in a given place and that it applies, first of all, to the local community assembled for eucharist instead of to a worldwide spiritual fellowship or to some worldwide institution. Faith in Jesus Christ has become such an individualistic matter that it is difficult to get across the idea that faith in Jesus Christ has a communal or corporate or ecclesial dimension which is expressed and fostered in the community's eucharist. Many people are completely unaware that the glorified Jesus is unrecognizable without us as his Spirit-filled Body—which the celebration of the eucharist is meant to embody. The often heard declaration that "I don't need to go to church; I can live a decent Christian life very well without it" speaks volumes. First of all, expressions of this sort show that the Christian life is easily equated with decent moral living. This is regrettable, for the first characteristic of a Christian life is that God has graced us in Jesus Christ. It is not what we have to show for ourselves that matters but the extent to which we have let this faith certainty define us. Second, this expression displays a mindset that is not well disposed towards the meaning of going to church described above. The point made in a third-century document deserves a favorable hearing:

> Whenever you are teaching, command and exhort the people to be faithful to the assembly of the church. Let them not fail to attend, but let them gather faithfully together. Let no one deprive the Church by staying away; if they do, they deprive the body of Christ of one of its members! For you must not think only of others but of yourself as well, when you hear the words that our Lord spoke: "Who does not gather with me, scatters" (Mt 12:30). Since you are the members of Christ, you must not scatter yourselves outside the Church by failing to assemble there. For we have Christ for our Head, as he himself promised and announced, so that "You have become sharers with us." Do not, then, make light of your own selves, do not deprive our Savior of his members, do not rend, do not scatter his Body.[3]

Does the concern expressed in this document still resonate with our perception of what it means to be a Christian or have typically twentieth-century socio-cultural factors such a hold on us that we find it difficult to share this concern?

One more element, the place and the role of the presiding minister in the eucharistic assembly, needs to be considered. When the community assembles as the Body of Christ in this place, it realizes that the one who really presides over the community's celebration of the eucharist is the risen Christ who, in the power of the Spirit, is the Head of his Body, the church. This presidency of Christ is visibly, that is sacramentally, expressed by the presiding minister. The Ministry section of the Faith and Order Commission's document *Baptism, Eucharist and Ministry* expresses this aspect very well:

> It is especially in the eucharistic celebration that the ordained ministry is the visible focus of the deep and all-embracing communion between Christ and the members of his body. In the celebration of the eucharist, Christ gathers, teaches and nourishes the Church. It is Christ who invites to the meal and who presides at it.[4]

This helps us to grasp the significance and functioning of the presiding minister in the context of the eucharist. His is indeed a sacramental role, namely, that in him the presidency of Christ over the community that has gathered in his name is made visible. This shows that the presiding minister, whose primary dignity, let us not forget, derives from the fact that he is baptized and confirmed, is a constitutive and integral part of the community. He can only be understood within and in relation to the assembled community. At the same time, the eucharistic community cannot function without the presence of the presiding minister who, in the words of the above document (no. 8) points to the church's fundamental dependence on Jesus Christ and thereby provides, within a multiplicity of gifts, a focus of its unity. This is why the presiding minister needs to be ordained. There are other aspects, such as the apostolicity and catholicity of the eucharistic community, that also dictate that the presider must be ordained, but it would lead us too far afield to develop them here. Suffice it to say, the presiding minister is one of the four elements of the eucharist.

We Assemble on the Day of the Lord

The eucharist can be and is celebrated in a great number of different settings on widely varying occasions. A funeral liturgy normally includes the eucharist for obvious reasons because if there is one time that we need to put our highest trump card, the paschal mystery of Christ, on the table it is in the face of death. When the eucharist is celebrated with great numbers of people during the frequent trips of the present pope, it is often identified as "the Papal Mass," a designation that we should use with caution, because it makes the presider too prominent. For some, daily eucharist is an indispensable element in their spiritual life. The eucharist is also frequently celebrated, when a group of Roman Catholics meet for a convention, for a retreat, for the opening of an academic year, for Cursillos, etc. There is also a "Red Mass," a "Police Mass," and so on, where secular groups, which include members who are not even baptized, lay claim to a Mass to highlight an event significant to their organization. This is an improper use of the Mass. Apart from the funeral liturgy, in many of these instances we may well wonder whether having recourse to the eucharist is not often too facile a solution because, with a bit of creativity and greater attentiveness to the church's liturgical repertoire, planners would discover that other forms of liturgy which are better suited to the particular situation are readily available. Needless to say, although the celebration of the eucharist is fundamentally the same, in these different circumstances it takes on a unique coloring depending on the particular setting in which it occurs.

I must say I have a bias for the celebration of the eucharist in a parish setting on a Sunday morning. This does not, of course, cancel out the legitimacy of the eucharist on other occasions. I believe, however, that the parish context provides the setting in which the eucharist has the best chance of being celebrated to its full capacity. This is not to suggest that in actual practice this potential is fully realized. Apart from the fact that the eucharist is celebrated rather poorly in some parishes, there are at least three factors that militate against the realization of the ideal. First, the immense size of some of our parishes makes it difficult to build a real sense of eucharistic community. Second, in a good number of parishes the need to accommodate the Sunday observance of individual parishioners has more to do with the scheduling of the eucharist than the desire to bring the eucharistic community together. Consequently there are more celebrations of the eucharist than a parish actually needs. This can have a negative effect both on our understanding of the eucharist and on what it means for us to be church. The third factor that prevents the eucharist from building this community of men and women into the Body of Christ is a recent phenomenon in our part of the world. An increasing number of viable parish communities must refrain from Sunday eucharist because of the absence of a priest. The implications of this are only slowly beginning to dawn on us.

Why favor the celebration of the eucharist in a parish setting on Sunday? While spelling out the basic directives for our understanding of the liturgical year, Vatican II's Constitution on the Sacred Liturgy says this of Sunday:

> By a tradition handed down from the apostles, which took its origin from the very day of Christ's resurrection, the Church celebrates the paschal mystery every seventh day, which day is appropriately called the Lord's Day or Sunday. For on this day Christ's faithful are bound to come together into one place. They should listen to the word of God and take part in the Eucharist, thus calling to mind the passion, resurrection, and glory of the Lord Jesus, and giving thanks to God who "has begotten them again, through the resurrection of Christ from the dead, unto a living hope" (I Pet. 1:3). The Lord's Day is the original feast day, and it should be proposed to the faithful and taught to them so that it may become in fact a day of joy and of freedom from work.[5]

It is not difficult to appreciate how important Sunday is for us Christians. When we consider that in the eucharist we are privileged to celebrate the paschal mystery of Christ from which we derive our identity as Body of Christ, it is hard to think of a more appropriate day to celebrate it. The Sunday celebration of Easter thus shapes the basic rhythm of the liturgical year, for on this day which is variously identified as the first day—because it is celebrated as the day of the new creation, of the new light, of the new life, the risen Christ—as the Day of the Lord—because it is the day on which we keep memorial of the Lord's resurrection—, as the eighth day—yet another designation to emphasize the beginning of a new creation—the Christian community needs to assemble to celebrate the resurrection of its Lord into which it is taken up. The Christological thrust of this day is best observed by the celebration of the Lord's Supper.

Although it is not my intention to discredit all the other occasions on which the eucharist is celebrated, there is an additional aspect which explains why the parish context on Sunday is the most favorable setting for its celebration. In the paschal mystery of Christ which is made effectively present in the celebration of the eucharist God has healed and reconciled a wounded and broken humanity. I like to think of the great variety of men and women who assemble for eucharist as a good sample of this wounded and broken humanity. But when they assemble for eucharist they become a sample of a healed and reconciled humanity. In their assembling for eucharist they become the visible expression of a humanity that is re-created in Christ. All possible division and distinctions are, for this hour at least, transcended and suspended. It may very well be that the divisions and distinctions will show up again afterwards, but in the eucharist these baptized-confirmed individuals tune into or plug into that grace-filled event, the paschal mystery of Christ, which alone can put an end to what divides us. Here, in the eucharistic assembly, if I may express it this way, "they play Kingdom," in the hope that they will be empowered to live a Kingdom life-style once they disperse. In this way they contribute to the healing and reconciliation of humanity. Is this what the apostle Paul had in mind when he felt it necessary to reproach the Corinthians for their uneucharistic-like behavior (1 Cor 11)?

Sunday, the Day of the Lord, and the eucharist belong together. There is evidence that the earliest generations of Christians were more aware of this self-evident link between Sunday and eucharist than we are. Sunday was considered to be the day on which the Christian community needed to come together to celebrate the death and resurrection of the Lord Jesus. Interestingly enough, as the third-century document mentioned earlier suggests, it was felt that, for the sake of the eucharistic community, Christians needed to come together. Non-participation in the eucharist was frowned upon and, in some instances, subject to disciplinary measures because it was felt to be a sign of disloyalty to the community as the Body of Christ.

We may detect here traces of a Sunday obligation, but with a communal and ecclesial emphasis. This is markedly different from the individualistic notion of Sunday obligation defined in moral terms which grew up in the course of the centuries. Going to Mass on Sunday came to be interpreted as an obligation towards

God. You owe it to God to worship for at least an hour a week. Not only does this represent a dangerously warped notion of worship—after all, worship in the Christian sense is not limited to a particular place but applies potentially to all of life, it also lacks a communal dimension. The result was that not going to Mass came to be understood as an offense against God and a serious sin. Thus we see a significant shift from the need of the community to assemble on the Day of the Lord for the celebration of the eucharist towards the need of the individual to observe his or her Sunday obligation by attending Mass. If today's liturgical reform is to achieve its purpose, then one of the things that must be done is to reverse this shift. In view of the important Christian values that are part of the intimate link between Sunday and eucharist, every effort made in this direction deserves support.

Notes

1. Alexander Schmemann, *The Eucharist, Sacrament of the Kingdom of God* (New York: St. Vladimir's Seminary Press, 1988) 11-27.

2. Ibid. 23.

3. *The Didascalia of the Apostles;* translation from Lucien Deiss, *Springtime of the Liturgy: Liturgical Texts of the First Four Centuries* (Collegeville: The Liturgical Press, 1979) 176-177.

4. *Baptism, Eucharist and Ministry,* Faith and Order Paper no. 111 (Geneva: World Council of Churches, 1982) no. 14.

5. Constitution on the Sacred Liturgy no. 106.

CHAPTER THREE

The Last Supper Narratives

Without suggesting that there is a neat linear progression from the New Testament accounts of the Last Supper to the church's Mass, I do think that to get a better understanding of the eucharist we must briefly consider these narratives. There is no need for us to delve into all sorts of technical details, but we must try to establish what portrait of Jesus is being sketched there. After all, the eucharist cannot be understood apart from the Jesus-event. He is the very content of the Last Supper narratives and of the church's eucharist. Moreover, the identity of the community that celebrates the eucharist is shaped by these narratives. We want to see who the Jesus at work here is so that we can better understand ourselves as a eucharistic community.

The quest for a better understanding of the eucharist through the study of the Last Supper narratives can be very rewarding, although it is easy to be overwhelmed by the plethora of books and articles professional exegetes have produced on the subject. Technical though much of their work may seem, these experts in Scripture make an indispensable contribution to the church. Without suggesting that other works are less useful, I would like to single out Xavier Léon-Dufour's *Sharing the Eucharistic Bread: The Witness of the New Testament*[1] which is particularly instructive

because he occasionally points out how the findings of professional exegetes can enrich our understanding of the eucharist.

The few verses taken, almost word for word, from the Last
Supper narratives which the presiding minister recites during the
central part of the eucharist, namely during the eucharistic prayer,
are of special interest. These particular verses have come to be
known as the institution narrative. Even though we realize that the
institution narrative functions adequately only within the context
of the entire eucharistic prayer and that for eucharist we need
more than the institution narrative, it has become such an intrinsic
and essential part of that prayer that the eucharist is unrecognizable without it. The institution narrative says a great deal about the
eucharist. In fact, it contains its most crucial aspects. But these
come to light only when we set the institution narrative in the
context of the Last Supper narratives from which it was taken.

Somehow, the trend that has been with us for many centuries
must be reversed. Our preoccupation with the real presence issue
has made us tend to isolate the words "This is my body" and "This
is my blood" even when we hear the institution narrative. Our
fixation on this issue has impoverished our understanding of the
eucharist to the point where, in the Western Church at least, the
isolated statements have come to be known as the words of
consecration. It is not that they cannot be understood this way, but
it does narrow the focus greatly and makes us lose sight of aspects
of the eucharist that are at least as important as the presence of
Christ in the consecrated bread and wine, if not more so. It is far
more rewarding if we set the institution narrative in the context of
the Last Supper narratives instead of zeroing in on these isolated
words. In its proper setting its immense significance stands out
clearly.

At this point some may wonder whether we are dealing with the
institution narrative as found in the eucharistic prayer or with the
Last Supper narratives as found in the Scriptures. Needless to say,
our primary interest is the institution narrative which has such a
strategic place in the all-important eucharistic prayer. But, for all
sorts of reasons, something happened to the institution narrative
in the course of the church's history that prevented it from fulfill-
ing its properly eucharistic function. There are two aspects to this.

32

First of all, the institution narrative suffered significantly from an over-all decline in the appreciation of the integrity of the eucharistic prayer. Only in this context can it play its unique eucharistic role. Strange as it may seem, the increasing prominence given to the institution narrative over the centuries at the expense of the integrity of the eucharistic prayer to which it belongs has been a real hindrance. As a consequence of its isolation the institution narrative came to be valued primarily for what it does to the bread and wine. This went to such extremes that some were even willing to argue that these words might have the same effect, even if recited outside of a properly eucharistic context. The question we must ask is: is the eucharistic function of the institution narrative to be sought in what it does to the bread and wine? Does it not play a more encompassing role than effecting the real presence of the body and blood of Christ in the consecrated bread and wine? The answer to this question comes to light when we are prepared to go back to the Last Supper narratives from which the institution narrative has been taken. In other words, the true significance of the institution narrative as part of the eucharistic prayer cannot be grasped adequately apart from the Last Supper narratives as found in the Scriptures.

The importance of the institution narrative is certainly not confined to the fact that it contains the words of consecration. In relation to the eucharist its primary function is to authorize the community to celebrate it. When we assemble for eucharist we do not engage in an activity that is properly our own but in something that the Lord Jesus does in his church. He, in the power of the Spirit, is the principal actor and he is actively present in the community that has assembled in his name. It is he who authorizes us to celebrate the eucharist. To bring this certainty of faith into focus is the properly eucharistic function of the institution narrative. This is why it is strategically placed in the eucharistic prayer. But, as the narrative that authorizes the eucharistic community to do eucharist, it will necessarily also contain the meaning of that eucharistic action, albeit in a condensed form. It is this meaning which we want to probe through a closer look at the Last Supper narratives. With the help of these narratives in the Synoptic Gospels (John handles the Last Supper scene quite differently) and

The Last Supper Narratives: A Comparison

Mt 26	Mk 14	Lk 22	1 Cor 11
20"When it was evening he was at table	17And when it was evening he comes	14And when the hour came he reclined at table	23On the night he was betrayed
with the Twelve [disciples]. 21And as	with the Twelve. And as	and the apostles with him. 15And he said to them:"I have greatly desired to eat this Passover with you before I suffer. 16For I tell you that I shall never eat it again until it is fulfilled, in the kingdom of God: 17And, having accepted a cup, having given thanks, he said: "Take this and share it among you. 18For I tell you that I shall not drink henceforth of the fruit of the vine until the reign of God comes."	
they were eating. . . .	they were at table and were eating. . . .		
26Now as they were eating, Jesus having taken bread and pronouncing the blessing, broke [it] and having given [it] to the disciples, said:	22And as they were eating, having taken bread, pronouncing the blessing, he broke [it], gave [it] to them and said:	19And having taken bread, having given thanks, he broke [it] and gave [it] to them, saying:	the Lord Jesus took bread 24and, having given thanks, broke [it] and said:

"Take, eat,
this is my body."

27And, having take
a cup

and having given thanks,
he gave [it] to them,

saying:
"Drink of it, all of you,
28for this is
my blood
of the covenant

which [is] shed
for the multitude
for the forgiveness of sins.
29I tell you,
henceforth I shall not drink
again
of this fruit of the vine until
that day when
I shall drink it new
with you in the
kingdom of my Father."

"Take,
this is my body."

23And, having taken
a cup,

having given thanks,
he gave [it] to them;
and they all drank of it.
24And he said to them:

"This is
my blood
of the covenant

which [is] shed
for the multitude.

25Truly, I tell you,
never more shall I drink

of the fruit of the vine
until that day when
I shall drink it new
in the
kingdom of God."

"This is my body

which [is] given for you.
Do this
in memory of me."

20And
the cup likewise
after the supper,

saying:

"This cup [is]

the new covenant
in my blood
which [is] shed
for you."

"This is my body

which [is] for you
Do this
in memory of me."

25Likewise also the cup
after the supper,

saying:

"This cup is

the new covenant
in my blood.

Do this, each time you drink
in memory of me."

26For each time that
you eat this bread
and drink this cup,
you proclaim the death of the
Lord until he comes.

know, at least in rudimentary fashion, what happened at the Last Supper, but we gain an insight into what is happening when the Church celebrates eucharist as authorized by its living Lord.

When taking a closer look at these Last Supper narratives, it should not surprise us that they are unintelligible without reference to the Old Testament. After all, as Christians we claim that God's grace-filled designs to which the Hebrew Scriptures bear witness find their fulfillment in the one whom we profess as Lord. So, where appropriate, we have to make reference to a few of the more significant Old Testament texts without which it is simply impossible to grasp what is happening not only at the Last Supper but in the church's eucharist as well.

The Meal Setting of the Last Supper Narratives

When we study the Last Supper narratives, one of the aspects that we must give due weight to is the meal setting. It is very significant that the domestic gesture of sitting at the same table and sharing bread and wine has been chosen as the vehicle for something that has the profoundest meaning for Christians. This influences both the portrait of Jesus sketched there and the identity of the community that celebrates. We must, therefore, pay attention to this setting. If we skip over this domestic gesture, we run the risk of not being able to get in touch with the profound reality of the eucharist.

Sharing a meal is one of those gestures we easily take for granted. What is immediately obvious about eating and drinking is that it has to do with life. We cannot do without it. This is the way life is sustained. At this physical level, eating and drinking are no different for us than they are for animals. But human beings give to the act of eating and drinking with others more than a biological significance and endow these acts with human meaning. We eat and drink with those with whom we have something in common to express and foster the bond that holds us together. Sharing a meal speaks of fellowship and bonding and communion among the participants. This is true of routine, everyday eating. It is even more true of meals on special occasions, such as birthdays, Thanksgiving, Christmas, etc. Naturally, on such occasions we appreciate the nutritional value of the food, but the sharing of it introduces a dynamic that influences the relationships of the participants. The success of the meal will be measured more by how it shapes these relationships than by the quality of the food.

We must go one step further and open up the potentially religious dimension of this domestic gesture. When this eating and drinking with others is done by believers, it should cause no surprise if God is brought into the picture. If life is sustained by food and drink, then it is appropriate that, in some way, we want to acknowledge the giver of life. By eating and drinking with others we want to acknowledge that the same God is the source of the fellowship and bonding which our shared meal is nourishing. This is ultimately the significance of "saying grace" before and/or after meals. It is a way of saying that God is the source of our life and our fellowship and that in our table fellowship we are in communion with God. The human action of eating and drinking takes on a religious meaning which is expressed in prayer.

There is an additional layer to this when the religious dimension of the meal is particularly prominent as it is, for example, in the Jewish Passover supper. Before the main course, the host presiding over the meal takes some bread, pronounces a short prayer of praise and thanksgiving to God over the bread, and then shares it with those who are about to participate in the meal. Similarly, after the meal, the one presiding takes a cup filled with wine, pronounces a somewhat more elaborate prayer of praise and thanksgiving which explains the reason for the thanksgiving. After the prayer the one presiding shares the cup with the participants. A beautiful example of this sort of prayer is the so-called *Birkat ha-mazon*:

> You are blessed, Lord our God,
>   King of the universe,
> you who nourish the entire world
> with goodness, tender love, and mercy.
>   You are blessed, O Lord,
> you who nourish the universe.
>
> We will give you thanks, Lord our God,
> for you have given us a desirable land for our inheritance,

that we may eat of its fruits
and be filled with its goodness.
You are blessed, Lord our God,
  for the land and the food.

Lord our God, take pity
on Israel your people and Jerusalem your city,
on Zion, the place where your glory dwells,
on your altar and your sanctuary.
You are blessed, O Lord, who build Jerusalem.
You are blessed, Lord our God,
  King of the universe,
you who are good and filled with kindness!

You are blessed, Lord our God,
  King of the universe,
you who are good and filled with kindness.[2]

A prayer like this gives voice to the participants' self- understanding in relation to the God from whom they receive their entire existence. We must keep the basic orientation and structure of this sort of prayer in mind because, even though the Christian community will thoroughly "Christologize" it by re-reading it from the perspective of the Jesus Christ event, it is the origin of the church's eucharistic prayer.

What we are particularly interested in is the significance of the brief ritual before and after the meal. It is more than an empty gesture. When the participants respond to the prayer pronounced by the presider with "Amen" and take some bread and a sip from the cup, the sharing of the bread and wine embodies the disposition of praise and thanksgiving all the participants have in common. In taking this bread and wine, the participants say that what the presider has articulated is their disposition as well, and they indicate that they want their lives to be lives of praise and thanksgiving.

We should keep this ritual and the basic thrust of the prayer in mind, because it helps us understand what Jesus does and says at the Last Supper: "Having taken bread and pronouncing the blessing" and "Likewise also the cup after the supper." Moreover, the eucharist was given its basic shape when the rituals before and after the meal were joined together. Eventually, the actual meal was skipped. We cannot, then, describe the eucharist as a full meal, although, of course, the meal character of these combined rituals remains perfectly intact.

These basic considerations of the Jewish meal setting are indispensable if we want to grasp the real significance of the Last Supper narratives. Obviously, the identity of the principal actor and the circumstances in which this particular meal takes place put a unique stamp on this ordinary domestic human action. The actions and the words of Jesus must be given careful attention, because they reveal how he reads the event. The words he uses during the human action of sharing a meal interpret its real meaning. In what he says, we get his version of what is really taking place.

When we let the accounts of the Last Supper speak for themselves, it immediately becomes obvious that they are a narrative of action and dialogue between Jesus and God, between Jesus and the disciples and, over the head of the disciples, between Jesus and ourselves who now celebrate the eucharist. Look at the dialogical thrust of the scene. Jesus converses and interacts with God and with his disciples. A meal setting, particularly one with an explicitly religious tone, provides the climate to evoke the profound reality of how Jesus relates to the disciples and how the disciples relate to God and one another because of their relationship to Jesus.

At the risk of appearing to be argumentative, I must insist that the focus of the narratives is not the bread and wine in themselves. This is true not only of the Last Supper narratives, but also of the institution narrative in the eucharist. The issue is not what happens to the bread and wine, but what happens to the disciples, and to us as disciples today, on account of what Jesus does and says in this particular meal setting. This point has to be made emphatically because in the past we have not sufficiently respected the uniqueness of the Last Supper narratives and, as a result, we have allowed our eucharistic reflections to be pulled somewhat off course.

It is only within the context of the important issue of what is happening between Jesus and the disciples that the bread and wine have their proper place. But even then, it is not the bread and wine as static objects which become important. It is the eating of this bread and the drinking of this wine that must be given full weight without losing sight of the fact that this eating and drinking are squarely situated within the dialogue that Jesus carries on with God and with his disciples. When we respect the structure and the basic flow of the Last Supper narratives, then it is immediately evident that the focus of attention is what is going on between Jesus and God and between Jesus and the disciples. It is in relation to this communication that the sharing of bread and wine takes on its proper meaning. This domestic gesture, in this particular setting, channels and expresses the relationship between Jesus and this community of disciples and the bond it creates between God and this assembly and between the members of the community. The consuming of this bread and wine is the bearer or the sacrament of the profound reality that the Last Supper narratives are trying to put into words. This is not simply so that we know what happened at the Last Supper. It is meant to cultivate a taste for what is really happening now when we as church celebrate the eucharist.

Three Horizons of the Last Supper Narratives

Isolating certain aspects from their proper context is dangerous. It impoverishes our understanding because it keeps the real significance of the isolated aspect from emerging. The lines "This is my body" and "This is my blood" are a case in point. We must, therefore, try to put them back into the Last Supper narratives, because it is only when they are seen within their proper context that the lines release their real meaning. But the same applies to the Last Supper narratives themselves. They, too, should not be isolated, lest we miss their true meaning. This can take us in different directions which have a bearing not only on the Last Supper narratives, but also on the celebration of the eucharist. For example, much comes to light when we associate the Last Supper narratives with the various table fellowship incidents that play such an important role in the Gospels either in the feeding of the multitude stories or in accounts of Jesus eating with sinners and tax collectors. These table fellowship incidents are not simply illustrations of Jesus eating. The feeding of the multitude stories evoke the idea that abundance of life is found in Jesus, whereas the accounts of Jesus eating with sinners and tax collectors convey and embody the idea that Jesus brings into communion with him those who tend to be excluded. For our purposes we can stay closer to the Last Supper narratives themselves, because they contain elements which we have ignored so far or not explicitly noted. I am particularly interested in what could be called the three horizons in which the Last Supper narratives stand. It is in light of these horizons and against their background that we can discover aspects of the Last Supper narratives which are not just interesting and intriguing, but are of the utmost importance for our understanding of the church's eucharist. Without them our understanding of the eucharist would be poorer and perhaps seriously distorted. One more caution: these three horizons must not be considered independently. They build on each other and it is their cumulative effect which gives us the most enriching insights into the eucharist.

The Passion Narrative Context

We do not find the Last Supper narratives just anywhere in the Gospels. Even Paul, in his First Letter to the Corinthians, calls up the event that not only hangs over this meal incident as a dark shadow but also shapes its significance. I am, of course, referring to the imminent death of Jesus. The story about the suffering and death of Jesus is the proper home for the Last Supper narratives, because they play an indispensable role there. In fact, without them we might not know how to understand the brutal event of his death. But Jesus' actions and words at the Last Supper not only give us his interpretation of what the sharing of this bread and wine mean. They also give us his interpretation of the violent death that is awaiting him the following day. Jesus' actions and words on the night before he is put to death lift his execution above the human level of murder by judicial process. His actions and words carry the meaning of sharing bread and wine and of the events of the following days and, over and above that, of the church's celebration of the eucharist.

41

The entire scene speaks of the imminent death of Jesus. But death is not just a biological event. Human beings have to understand death primarily in relational terms, because it is about separation and the lack of relationships. The actions and words of Jesus must be seen, therefore, as evoking and bringing about something that is diametrically opposed to what can be superficially observed. In the midst of a scene that speaks of separation, the meal setting and what Jesus does and what he says to his disciples speak of communion and fellowship. Here as in the entire Passion narratives, the path that leads to death is the path that leads to life in all its fullness, not only for Jesus himself but for all who believe in him.

Indeed, much is contained in the deliberate gestures and the carefully crafted words of Jesus. The gestures are familiar from the ordinary meal setting, but the words are new. They give the gestures a new meaning and a new content. In the words that accompany the gesture of sharing bread and wine, Jesus sums up the basic thrust of his entire life. What is expressed in his words is entirely in character with his life style. His life is marked by a total giving of self in obedience to God and in service to others. Unreserved faithfulness and love are the hallmarks of his life's orientation. When received by God, this life becomes the ground on which the communion and fellowship that the gestures and the words speak of become possible in a new and unheard of way. Because the self-giving of Jesus is received by the Father, it becomes the source of life and fellowship for the disciples. Therefore, inasmuch as the gestures and the words at the Last Supper are Jesus' own interpretation of the brutal events that are still to come, they speak of Jesus' basic disposition in life which was a giving of self motivated by faithful witness to God and the desire to be in communion with his disciples. "This is I as I give myself entirely so that you may live."

The words that accompany the gesture of sharing the cup filled with wine are extremely significant in this regard. There is, first of all, the fact that wine itself conjures up joy and, in a Hebrew context especially, it refers to one of the most sought-after Messianic gifts. appreciation of wine. But when Jesus, in connection with passing the cup filled with wine, uses words like blood and covenant, we must be very attentive. We are not dealing with anatomy here. Blood is virtually synonymous with life because without it there is no life. Blood is also related to the communion of life. But blood, precisely because it is the soul of life, belongs to God, the giver of all life. When we keep in mind that in the words associated with the sharing of the cup Jesus interprets the events of the following day, we find here the most powerful expression of what is at stake in his death. Yes, Jesus is put to death. But no one takes his life from him. He lays it down himself. The shedding of his blood, the violent death which taken by itself is a murderous act, has been transformed by Jesus into the eminent gesture of the giving of his life for our sake. Only love can do this. But this violent death freely accepted out of fidelity to the Father and out of love for us is for a very specific purpose. It is so that we as his disciples may find life in fullness. Where is life in fullness to be found but in communion with God? Thus the pouring out of his blood establishes covenant between God and us. In his life of faithfulness and service seen through to the end we find the stuff that enables us to live in communion with God and with each other. The central figure of the Last Supper scene is Jesus indeed, but Jesus portrayed as the Suffering Servant, the enigmatic figure that the prophet Isaiah speaks about. It is, in fact, one of the Suffering Servant songs that provides the basic inspiration for what the New Testament has Jesus say about himself at the Last Supper:

> See, my servant shall prosper;
> he shall be exalted and lifted up, and shall be very high.
> . . . .
> He was despised and rejected by others;
> a man of suffering and acquainted with infirmity;
> and as one from whom others hide their faces
> he was despised, and we held him of no account.
> Surely he has borne our infirmities and carried our diseases;
> yet we accounted him stricken, struck down by God, and afflicted.
> But he was wounded for our transgressions,
> crushed for our iniquities;
> upon him was the punishment that made us whole,
> and by his bruises we are healed.

43

. . . . .
Yet it was the will of the Lord to crush him with pain.
When you make his life an offering for sin,
he shall see his offspring, and shall prolong his days;
through him the will of the Lord shall prosper.
Out of his anguish he shall see light;
he shall find satisfaction through his knowledge.
The righteous one, my servant, shall make many righteous,
and he shall bear their iniquities.
Therefore I will allot him a portion with the great,
and he shall divide the spoil with the strong;
because he poured out himself to death,
and was numbered with the transgressors;
yet he bore the sin of many,
and made intercession for the transgressors (Isaiah 52:13;
53:3-5, 10-12).

It is on account of this Suffering Servant that the reality which prevents us from living in communion with God, namely our sinfulness, is removed.

Needless to say, something momentous happens to the disciples when they respond to the urging of Jesus to "take and eat," to "take and drink." They receive more than a piece of bread and a sip of wine. It is the self-giving of Jesus that they receive, a self-giving that is mediated in the sharing of bread and wine and that issues forth into a new community that knows itself anchored in Jesus and privileged to live from his gift. Their being in communion with Jesus transforms them into his Body. If then, subsequent to the Last Supper and after the actual death and resurrection of Jesus, the community of disciples performs the same meal action in memory of Jesus, the community knows that for its true identity it is totally dependent on that self-giving of Jesus, which is made effectively present in the context of the community's eucharist.

It should, therefore, be quite evident that the Last Supper narratives read in the light of the passion narratives tell us a great deal about the significance of the church's eucharist. But we have not yet articulated other aspects of the Last Supper narratives, and consequently of the eucharist, that come to light when we pay attention to the other contexts. These other aspects are not opposed to or entirely different from the one that surfaces from the passion narratives context. On the contrary, they build on it and complete it.

The Jewish Passover Context

Some scholars still debate whether the Last Supper was indeed a Passover meal. Whether it was or not, there is enough evidence to conclude that the Last Supper took place at Passover time and that the Passover motive had a hand in the shaping of the Last Supper narratives. The Passover atmosphere is very evident. Why mention this? Because it lays bare yet another constitutive feature of the church's eucharist.

If there is a night that can be called holy, it is the night of Passover. The Passover meal celebrated by the Jews—and Jesus and his first disciples are all Jews, and, therefore, they draw their religious identity from the Hebrew Scriptures—conjures up a twofold deliverance. The Jewish Passover is unthinkable without the deliverance from slavery in Egypt, the entrance into the Promised Land, and the constitution of the people as God's holy people. This foundational event constitutes the real content of the Jewish Passover celebrations. But the celebration of the Passover now also contains a future dimension inasmuch as this foundational event holds the promise and hope-filled expectation of the deliverance Israel will know in the coming of the Messiah who will fully reveal God's glory. The past deliverance celebrated now makes the Jews look forward to an even more glorious deliverance.

We are broadening the scope of the Last Supper narratives beyond the context of the story of the passion. However enlightening it is to see them in that setting, we cannot narrowly limit their significance to that context. The covenant that God initiated with Israel through his servant Moses and to which he remains faithful also holds the key to an important dimension of the death and resurrection of Jesus and, therefore, to the church's eucharist as well. The Passover of Jesus which gives us our Christian life and identity does not cancel out the Jewish Passover. In fact, despite the newness of this Passover, it presupposes the ancient Passover and builds on it. As Christians we claim that the Passover of Jesus

45

completes and fulfills the Passover that is the foundation of Israel's identity. There is an element of continuity and an element of discontinuity marking the unique relationship between the two.

The element of continuity is quite recognizable in the formulation of the words over the cup in the version of Matthew and Mark. Look at the similarity between these words and the words used for the sealing of the covenant with the Hebrew people:

> Moses took half of the blood and put it in basins, and half of the blood he dashed against the altar. Then he took the book of the covenant, and read it in the hearing of the people; and they said, "All that the Lord has spoken we will do, and we will be obedient." Moses took the blood and dashed it on the people, and said, "See the blood of the covenant that the Lord has made with you in accordance with all these words" (Ex 24:6-8).

Paul's and Luke's versions, on the other hand, advocate the element of discontinuity when they insist that this is a *new* covenant. Their version is inspired by the text of the prophet Jeremiah:

> The days are surely coming, says the Lord, when I will make a new covenant with the house of Israel and the house of Judah. It will not be like the covenant that I made with their ancestors when I took them by the hand to bring them out of the land of Egypt—a covenant that they broke, though I was their husband, says the Lord. But this is the covenant that I will make with the house of Israel after those days, says the Lord: I will put my law within them, and I will write it on their hearts; and I will be their God, and they shall be my people. No longer shall they teach one another, or say to each other, "Know the Lord," for they shall all know me, from the least of them to the greatest, says the Lord, for I will forgive their iniquity, and remember their sin no more" (31:31-34).

The covenant is new inasmuch as it is sealed not with the blood of animals, but with the self-giving of Jesus, the Servant of Yahweh.

The more technical notion of *anamnesis, memorial, remembrance* needs to be introduced here. The recovery of this biblical notion has been extremely important and has provided new openings for an ecumenical discussion on the eucharist. There is a unique Judeo-Christian way of remembering. It is a remembering that holds past, present, and future together. The past foundational event is remembered with thanksgiving because it enables us to deal with our present-day concerns in such a way that a hope-filled perspective on the future is opened up. This sort of remembering has nothing to do with thinking about the good old days or with being respectful towards the past. It is a remembering that brings the event remembered into the present so that it can serve as a springboard towards the future.

This sense of remembering certainly applies to both the Jewish and the Christian Passover. Applied to the Jewish Passover, it means that God's great deed of setting Israel free from slavery is remembered, celebrated, and proclaimed so that those who do the remembering can be present to that event and even more to the God who liberates and saves and whose name and face they know on the basis of the event remembered. When the foundational event is recalled, what is really remembered is the principal actor, that is to say the God of the Exodus, the God who sets free. God's great deed is remembered because it gives the people a foundation for their confidence and trust in God's future deed of deliverance. When Jesus, in that Passover atmosphere, says "Do this in memory . . . of me," we are confronted with the immense claim that Jesus and the Christian community make. The "of me" is the startlingly new element. All humanity has been delivered from the slavery of death and everything that smells of death, above all, sin—"in me," the new Moses who experiences his Passover from death to life on behalf of all. What we are confronted with is the claim that God's promise to deliver us has become reality in the life, death, and resurrection of Jesus. This is the Passover that the Christian community remembers. But, obviously, the future dimension so prominent in the Hebrew way of remembering is not absent from the Christian remembering. We make the claim that the Messiah has come in Jesus dead and risen but, without suggesting that it is a half truth at best, there is just too much evidence that this coming of the Messiah has not had its desired effect on the world he is supposed to have saved. So we too look forward to the coming in glory of this risen Jesus. While remembering with gratitude the

47

coming of the Messiah, we look forward with hope and anticipation to his coming in glory. Come, Lord Jesus. Come!

The remembering that we as a Christian community engage in when we celebrate the eucharist, authorized by the "Do this in memory of me," effectively makes present the paschal mystery—the life, death, and resurrection of Jesus Christ—in such a way that it shapes our lives and becomes, in fact, our paschal mystery. When we share bread and wine in memory of Jesus, we are put in the presence of the saving event of the cross and participate in the new life of the Risen Jesus. The Spirit-filled bread and wine become the heavenly food and drink that sustain the church as the Body of Christ and empower this Body of Christ to continue the saving, liberating, and reconciling ministry of its Lord.

The Kingdom of God Horizon

The third horizon emerging from a close reading of the Last Supper Narratives in their entirety is that of the Kingdom of God. That is the ultimate reality by which Jesus allowed himself to be claimed, the reality that he lived for and for which he was prepared to die. The whole life-story of Jesus must be understood in terms of this reality. It is the principal motive of his entire ministry. Jesus spoke of its imminence when he began his ministry. It is the favored topic of his many parables. We see its in-breaking in the miracles he performs, miracles that are not so much sensational acts as signs and hints of what it will be like when God indeed reigns. No wonder, then, that Jesus cannot keep silent about the Kingdom when his death is imminent. When, from a human point of view, his life is about to end in failure, from God's perspective, the Kingdom is about to burst forth. An immense paradox indeed. God's wisdom and power stand fully revealed in human foolishness and defeat. When everything speaks of death, Jesus dares to speak of life in all its fullness, for that is what the Kingdom of God is all about.

Matthew and Mark have Jesus speak of that Kingdom at the end of the Last Supper narratives, whereas Luke mentions it at the very beginning. In Paul's version it is suggested in the "until he comes." What breaks through is the so-called eschatological perspective. The broadest possible scope of the Last Supper scene and of the eucharist is being evoked: how things will be in the end-time. Then we will sit with the Lord at the Messianic Banquet and delight in the meal of the Kingdom of God. That eschatological perspective is already present in the gestures and words that accompany the sharing of the bread and wine, when we come together on the basis of his self-giving to share in the messianic table fellowship with the Lord Jesus. But by mentioning the Kingdom of God Jesus makes it even more explicit. He makes his disciples look forward to the Kingdom that will finally be inaugurated by his death and by the resurrection from the dead that will make him the cornerstone of it.

But note carefully what the Synoptic Gospels have Jesus say of the eating and drinking of the fruit of the vine. He will only do it again when the Kingdom of God has come. This would seem to mean that, when we as a community of his disciples share bread and wine in memory of Jesus, we are privileged to anticipate the Messianic Banquet, the meal of the Kingdom. When we celebrate eucharist we, as it were, "jump the gun," we "play Kingdom." It is a dimension of the eucharist that we have never contradicted or denied. Rather, it has remained dormant; we have not been very conscious of it for centuries. The memory of his death as a past event has been so dominant that it has virtually blocked our vision of the future that his death actually opened up for us. Losing sight of that broader scope or horizon has resulted in the eucharist being seen as a remembrance of the death of Jesus only. Of course, the recovery of that eschatological dimension of the eucharist does not allow us to go to the other extreme as though we can harmlessly celebrate the future while skipping over the past and the present. This would make the eucharist into something entirely unreal. No, in the eucharist we anticipate the fulfillment of the Kingdom to which the death and resurrection of the Lord Jesus give us access in the present, but in such a way that we can handle our present day concerns, both the positive and the negative ones, with hope.

None of these aspects mentioned remain limited solely to the Last Supper narratives. They all find their way into the celebration of the eucharist by the Christian community. This indicates, at the minimum, that when the Christian community assembles for eucharist it is not dealing with something marginal to the Christian life or the church's identity. On the contrary, it should be quite evident that we are dealing with the foundation of who we are as church. The church's eucharist is indeed an overwhelmingly rich reality, so rich in fact that not all dimensions can be held equally in view at all times. In one period in the church's history one aspect may have more prominence than another. Allowance must be made for that, as long as the prominence given to one feature does not lead to a certain forgetfulness about the other aspects or, worse still, to making virtually exclusive claims with reference to the particular aspect favored. A going back to the sources—and what more authoritative source is there than the Last Supper narratives?—can prevent this or, where called for, can help us make the necessary corrections so that the wealth of the eucharist will be seen more clearly. That was why we wrestled with the Last Supper narratives a bit.

And John?

We have been dealing with the Last Supper narratives as found in the Synoptic Gospels and in Paul's First Letter to the Corinthians because these versions have found their way into the church's eucharist. They provide the basic outline for what has come to be known as the institution narrative in the eucharistic prayer. The Gospel of John also speaks of the Last Supper of Jesus with his disciples, but in a significantly different way. John uses the Last Supper scene as the setting in which Jesus pronounces the immensely moving and powerful farewell discourse and high priestly prayer. He also makes it the setting in which he relates an incident that may appear to be quite different from the meal that Jesus has with his disciples in the Synoptic Gospels. In reality, however, when it comes to the basic meaning of that incident we soon discover that it is the same Jesus with the very same intentions who is at work here. We are, of course, referring to the incident of Jesus washing the feet of his disciples. Here, too, Jesus makes himself into the servant of others in order to bring his disciples into communion with him. Jesus commands his disciples to wash the feet of others. In other words, the disciples can remember the

Servant Jesus by becoming the servants of others. Yes, as a community of disciples of Jesus we must remember Jesus by sharing bread and wine in his memory. But to keep that more ritual way of remembering Jesus honest and authentic, it must be matched by a more existential and concrete way of remembering Jesus, namely in the form of life-giving service to others.

There is another place in John's Gospel where we find echoes of the Last Supper narratives more in line with the Synoptic presentation. It is in chapter six, in the more explicitly eucharistic section (vs. 51-58) of the Bread of Life discourse. What is particularly revealing is the way the eucharistic section is built into the broader and even more fundamental issue of accepting Jesus in faith as the one sent by the Father so that we may have the life that comes from being in communion with God. It is one more indication of how central the eating and drinking of the eucharistic bread and wine is to Christian identity. This eating and drinking is not an isolated gesture but the concrete way in which we adhere in faith to him who identifies himself as the bread from heaven.

Notes

1. Xavier Léon-Dufour, *Sharing the Eucharistic Bread: The Witness of the New Testament* (New York: Paulist Press, 1987).

2. *Birkat ha-mazon* in Lucien Deiss, *Springtime of the Liturgy: Liturgical Texts of the First Four Centuries* (Collegeville: The Liturgical Press, 1979) 7-8.

CHAPTER FOUR

One Single Act of Worship Made up of Two Closely Connected Parts

The principal contention of these theological reflections on the eucharist is that an adequate theology of the eucharist can be constructed on the basis of the fourfold presence of Christ in the eucharist: in the community assembled, in the presiding minister, in the word proclaimed, and in the bread and wine which are shared after the prayer of praise and thanksgiving has been proclaimed over them. If we pay attention to the basic liturgical rite as a whole and X-ray it with the eyes of faith, we see that the outline of a eucharistic theology flows from the very activities in which this assembled and structured community engages. This community of baptized-confirmed men and women has assembled primarily because of its faith in the living Lord Jesus who is actively present in its midst.

Apart from other gestures, activities, and interactions, the community assembled in his name has basically two rallying points in the eucharistic setting: the Scriptures and the bread and wine. The community huddles around the Scriptures and around the bread and wine. These are the two poles of its eucharistic action, but not in a static objectified sense. The focus is not on the Bible and the bread and wine themselves but on what the community does with and around them: the Scriptures are proclaimed and listened to and the bread and wine over which praise and thanksgiving to

God has been given are shared. These are the other two elements of the eucharist mentioned earlier. The community assembled is nourished at the table of the word and at the table of the eucharistic bread and wine.

Before we reflect on each of the two elements in more detail, we must underline that they belong together and that they constitute the eucharist in the comprehensive sense. The General Instruction of the Roman Missal states: "The Mass is made up as it were of the liturgy of the word and the liturgy of the eucharist, two parts so closely connected that they form but one single act of worship."[1] If it is the Body of Christ that has assembled for eucharist, then it is quite appropriate to suggest that it is with these two lungs that this body breathes, and for the health of the body it is of the greatest importance that both lungs are in good working condition and that both are, in fact, used.

It is important to make this point because we are just coming out of a roughly four hundred year-long experience in which the divided Body of Christ has tried to get by with only one lung. This may be an oversimplification, because there are, no doubt, other factors that account for the tragic and scandalous division that has weighed down and, unfortunately, still weighs down Western Christianity. We are, of course, referring to the sixteenth-century split that rent the Body of Christ asunder into the Roman Catholic Church, on the one hand, and the Reformation Churches, on the other. When we try to describe that tragic and scandalous split in terms of eucharistic practice, it seems legitimate to suggest that the Roman Catholic Church tried to breathe with one lung by trying to live almost exclusively from the sacrament proper, that is to say, from what it claimed takes place around the bread and wine. The Reformation Churches, on the other hand, tried to breathe with the other lung by insisting on the importance of the word to such an extent that they tended to play down the importance of the sacrament proper.

The Roman Catholic Church never abandoned the practice of reading from the Scriptures in the context of the eucharist. But the selection of the Scripture readings was so limited that we would be hard pressed to maintain that the Scriptures really held a prominent place in our understanding of the eucharist. They simply were not an integral part of Roman Catholic eucharistic consciousness. There is considerable evidence for that. The virtual absence of any serious theological reflection on that part of the Mass in the elaborate and voluminous theological treatises on the eucharist of that period is striking. It was also quite evident when there was a sermon in the context of a Mass. Rarely was the preaching based on the actual day's scripture readings. The church's teaching on faith and morals provided the sermon's content. Moreover, this preaching was not done from the place where the Scriptures were read. From a very practical point of view, coming late for or actually missing this part of the Mass was not considered very sinful. The focus was clearly on what we today would consider the second part of the Mass.

In the Reformation Churches, on the other hand, there was a trend in the opposite direction. Precisely in reaction to Roman Catholic developments, they tended to insist so much on the word that their Sunday worship, which included hymns and prayers, focused on the reading from the Scriptures and, especially, on the subsequent sermon. In many of their churches the celebration of the Lord's Supper or Holy Communion was considered to be an adjunct to the real worship service.

The tragedy is not simply that one side neglected the word and that the other side neglected the sacrament proper. It is more serious than that. The real tragedy is that the part emphasized is seriously impoverished, if not in fact distorted, because the sacrament cannot do without the word nor the word without the sacrament. If faith aroused by preaching based on the Scriptures does not inform the ritual of bread and wine, then it is very difficult to keep the latter from turning into something magical. Similarly, if preaching does not lead to and find its complement in the ritual, then the preaching runs the risk of becoming verbose, didactic, or moralizing. In other words, the part emphasized actually suffers when a loss of balance interferes with its healthy interaction with the part neglected. This is the rather sorry state of affairs in which the two sides of Western Christianity have found themselves for a number of centuries. One side has leaned on the sacrament proper and the other has leaned on the word to such an extent that they have almost separated two elements that for the health of the

One Body of Christ need to be held together so they can interact and nourish each other.

As a result of the liturgical renewal that has taken place in this century, both sides are making a serious attempt to retrieve the element they have long neglected. This is very encouraging and exciting. We finally are beginning to breathe with two lungs again. On our side, we are beginning to recover the importance of the liturgy of the word which, if we heed the official teaching of our church articulated in the above quotation from the General Instruction, should be considered an integral and constitutive part of the Mass. In many Reformation Churches, on the other hand, we witness the recovery of the sacrament proper in the form of a more frequent celebration of the eucharist. In many instances, this is according to a revised ritual.

This recovery is not automatic, of course. Many ingrained habits and considerable prejudice must be overcome. It is not only a matter of giving due weight to the part neglected for so long. It also implies the need and the willingness to make adjustments in the part that was emphasized because, in the polemical climate in which we felt the need to prove the other side wrong, patterns developed that were not conducive to an integral and comprehensive understanding of precisely that section of the Mass. If I may be permitted another image: if we have been limping on one leg for four centuries, considerable adjustment is called for when we learn to walk on two legs again. From a Roman Catholic perspective, we should not be surprised to discover, as a result of the eucharistic liturgy properly interacting with the liturgy of the word, that the eucharistic liturgy contains and reveals aspects that went unnoticed when it was dealt with in virtual isolation.

At this point it might be helpful to make a brief sketch of what I consider the basic characteristics of the two parts that constitute the church's eucharist. In subsequent chapters I intend to unpack what is presented here in a rudimentary fashion. What is immediately evident in this sketch is the descending and ascending movement in the overall structure of the eucharist. This is no coincidence, if we consider what is at stake in the church's liturgy.

The eucharist is one single act of worship made up of two closely connected parts:

In the first part:

We come together as God's people to let ourselves be addressed and nourished by the word of God;

- This liturgy of the word shows that Christianity is a revelation religion based on God's self-communication witnessed to in the Scriptures.
- The Sunday Lectionary orders the scripture readings not as a lesson plan but in function of
  — what the community is: the Body of Christ;
  — what the community celebrates: the paschal mystery of Christ, the source of its identity as the Body of Christ.
- Preaching
  — is bound by the scripture readings;
  — and leads the community
    + to praise and thank God;
    + to "find a home" in the mystery that is being celebrated.

In the second part:

Over bread and wine we give thanks and praise to the Father for what God has done for us in the self-giving of Jesus and what the Spirit continues to do among us: establishing covenant with us and among us in Jesus the Christ.

- That self-giving of Jesus is effectively made present among us in a sacramental way,
  — when, on the part of God, the paschal mystery of Christ is made present in the power of the Spirit
  — and when, on our part, we partake in faith of the bread and wine, the body and blood of Christ.
- When we share the body and blood of Christ,
  — we are transformed into the Body of Christ which makes us a living sacrifice of praise, agents of God's work of transforming the world into the Kingdom;
  — we receive a foretaste of the Messianic Banquet.

Note

1. General Instruction of the Roman Missal 7.

CHAPTER FIVE

The Liturgy
of the Word

When the Christian community assembles for worship it is conscious of the fact that it has not assembled on its own initiative. It has been brought together by the God who calls and summons. This God who calls and summons is not some anonymous Supreme Being. God is the God whose name, face, and identity have come to be known to us in the history of Israel which reaches a climax in the story of Jesus of Nazareth whom we Christians profess to be the truest son of Israel and acclaim as Lord. God is the God of Abraham and Sarah, of Moses, David, and Mary; the God and Father of Jesus Christ the Lord, the God whom, in Jesus Christ and in the power of the Spirit, we are privileged to call our God and Father. But the name, face, and identity of this God is not yet fully known, because only when the Lord Jesus comes in glory will he be fully revealed. In the interim period of "the already" and "the not yet" we assemble in the name of the Lord Jesus who is so present in our midst that we know ourselves, as an assembled community and in the power of the Spirit, to be the Body of Christ. The opening rites of the eucharist serve to bring this awareness into focus. This is the basic principle of all Christian liturgy since liturgy is the stage on which Christian identity, which cannot be found apart from Jesus Christ, is acted out.

This is true not only of the initial moments of our assembling as the Body of Christ but of the whole eucharist. It is very evident in the first part of the eucharist where we place ourselves before the word of God contained in the Scriptures. This is part of what makes the Christian faith unique. We gather, we "huddle" around the word of God that has taken on human form in the person of Jesus Christ. We do not come together around some insightful and inspirational readings that lift our hearts and minds to God. Our identity as Body of Christ does not depend on the penetrating insights of some religious genius. Our Christian identity is entirely dependent on God's self- communication to us in the history of Israel. This revelation reaches its climax in the life, death, and resurrection of Jesus. This, in the final analysis, is what the seventy-three different writings that make up the Bible bear faithful and authoritative witness to. The source of our Christian identity is the grace-filled initiative of God who in Jesus Christ makes himself into our God and us into his people. This, admittedly, raises some delicate issues that have recently surfaced as a consequence of the increasing and constructive encounter with other religions. How can Christians enter into authentic dialogue with representatives of other religions for the purpose of seeking truth when they profess Jesus Christ as the one in whom God is fully revealed and through whom all may have access to God? This is not the place to deal with these new and difficult questions. For the moment it is enough to say that, without any intended sense of exclusiveness or superiority, the Judeo-Christian Scriptures bear authoritative witness to God's loving design for all of humanity and that, as Christians, without any merits of our own, we have been privileged to respond to this in faith.

This is why the first part of the eucharist is a liturgy of the word. By having recourse to the Scriptures we make an important faith statement. By placing the Scriptures first and foremost, we honor the primacy of God's word in the community, because we know only too well that nothing exists apart from God's word. We owe our existence to God's creative word. God has spoken his word of salvation throughout all history in a great variety of ways, but God's creative and salvific word finally took on flesh in Jesus. It is no coincidence that, precisely at the most crucial junctures of the

Bible, primacy is given to the word God speaks: the opening verses of the Bible, the beginning of Israel's history in the calling of Abraham, the calling of the prophets Isaiah and Jeremiah, the beginning of John's Gospel, the opening lines of the letter to the Hebrews. God's utterance of his word, as witnessed to in the Scriptures, has several characteristics that make it into a unique speaking of this God. God's very identity is contained and revealed in this speaking. God's word accomplishes what it says. It establishes a covenant between God and the hearers who are likewise covenanted to one another. It builds up and fashions God's people. It exposes people's darker and sinful side and summons them to conversion. It is a word of promise and hope. Those same characteristics apply as well to the readings of the Scriptures in the context of the church's worship, when the community of disciples assembles to act out its unique relationship with its God in ritual-symbolic form. Obviously, then, the liturgy of the word in the context of the eucharist is not the consequence of some arbitrary decision, but something dictated by the logic of the Christian faith.

The primacy of the word God speaks is also observed in the community's attitude and response. It listens to, assimilates, and appropriates the word that is being proclaimed. This listening is a receptive activity that shapes the community into the obedience of faith. As church we are a listening people who live on what comes from the mouth of God. We, like Israel, are commanded: "Listen, Israel: Yahweh our God is the one, the only Yahweh. You must love Yahweh your God with all your heart, with all your soul, with all your strength. Let the words I enjoin on you today stay in your heart" (Dt 6:4-6). When we come together as God's people, we let ourselves be addressed and nourished by the word of God, the living Christ "who speaks when the holy scriptures are read in the Church."[1] No wonder, then, that the Scriptures have pride of place in the first part of the community's eucharist.

The Sunday Lectionary

Needless to say, the Scriptures can be read in a variety of ways. But when we have assembled for eucharist there is a certain

61

pattern to the reading that is conditioned by what this assembled community is doing. Not just any reading from the Scriptures will do. Rather, we have recourse to what could be called a liturgical reading of the Bible. The Sunday lectionary is an ordered system of selected readings from the Bible designed for liturgical use in the Sunday celebration of the eucharist. The arrangement of the biblical texts is determined by their liturgical use. It means that the lectionary is not the best place to look for some sort of a lesson plan for a classroom setting or an arrangement of texts for Bible study sessions. The readings can, of course, be used for these purposes, but they work best in the context of the church's worship.

The Sunday lectionary in use in the Roman Catholic Church since 1969 is vastly different from the one that preceded it. The previous Sunday lectionary gave us only two readings from the Scriptures for each celebration, the same readings occurred every year and all were from the New Testament. The present Sunday lectionary offers us three readings. The first is taken from the Hebrew Scriptures or the Old Testament (except for Easter time, when the first reading is chosen from the Acts of the Apostles) and is followed by a psalm. The second reading is from one of the letters in the New Testament or the Book of Revelation, and the third from one of the four Gospels. Since the new Sunday lectionary follows a three-year cycle, the sets of scripture readings recur only every third year. In spite of the inevitable flaws, the arrangement of the readings has been done so well that a good number of non-Roman Catholic Churches have made the appropriate modifications and adopted the lectionary for their worship services. Imagine the immense ecumenical significance of having virtually all Christian Churches in the English speaking world placing themselves before the same scripture readings each Sunday.

The assumptions on which the Sunday lectionary is built may be more important than its actual shape. After all, it is not the result of a random throwing together of biblical readings but the product of some basic principles of which the most important one has already been mentioned, namely that the Sunday lectionary is a liturgical reading of the Bible. A familiarity with these principles will enhance our appreciation of the lectionary and help us to use it better.

The reform of the church's Sunday lectionary is not some isolated incident standing on its own. We can only appreciate the significance of the revised Sunday lectionary when we see it as a sub-section of the eucharistic reform mandated and set in motion by Vatican II. If one aspect of eucharistic reform is to make the assembled community understand that it is the Body of Christ and that the eucharist is the activity of the entire assembly, it follows that the revised lectionary is meant to help the assembly celebrate and manifest that Christ is present in his Body. That is to say that the decisive factor in the choice of the scripture passages has been the faith conviction that Jesus Christ, the living Lord, is at the center of the community that celebrates the eucharist. This eucharistic setting is crucial and that is why, although the other readings are not devalued, the gospel reading is the dominant or controlling text in this set of readings. An important consequence of this eucharistic setting is that, when the scripture readings of the Sunday lectionary are proclaimed in this format but not followed by the liturgy of the eucharist, justice is not done to this arrangement of Scripture.

What gives the Sunday lectionary its basic unity and rhythm is the foundational character of the community's weekly celebration of the redemptive mystery of Christ. This celebration on the Lord's Day endows the church with its true identity. The lectionary unfolds the paschal mystery of Christ not as a past event but as the ground of the community's identity as the Body of Christ celebrated here and now. This, too, is unique to a reading of the Scriptures in the context of the church's eucharist. In the proclamation of the readings, which is itself a liturgical act, we are not simply being informed about past events. We have recourse to the written record of how people in the past have experienced God in the hope that we may discern how this God is salvifically at work in this assembled community and be able, consequently, to respond to God in faith. In other words, the liturgical reading of the Bible is set within the experience of our encounter with the salvific intentions God has for us. Therefore, the church assembles on Sunday not to commemorate the past event of Christ's death and resurrection but to celebrate that this paschal mystery of Christ now takes place in the assembled community. This is based on the faith certainty that in rising from the dead Jesus raised up a new community in the Spirit. In the same vein, the gospel stories are not simply good memories about a Jesus imprisoned in the past, but stories of the church in its saving encounter with its risen Lord. The scripture readings, and especially the Gospel, are selected in order to help the assembled community enter more deeply into the paschal mystery of Christ so that Christ's story might indeed become its story.

The Sunday lectionary, therefore, is Christocentric because each Sunday the church celebrates the paschal mystery of Christ. That is its primary focus. But this Christ mystery is, in a sense, so massive and so all-encompassing that it needs to be unfolded in an annual pattern. The liturgical year, which has Easter as its focus, is shaped to help us celebrate the all- important mystery of Christ from which we draw our identity. This means that the weekly rhythm, which is primary, is complemented by an annual rhythm so that, at a more leisurely pace, we may be grafted deeply into Christ crucified, risen, and present in our midst in the power of the Spirit. This celebration of Easter, which stands at the core of the liturgical year and for which we prepare by a Lenten journey of forty days, is really a fifty-day (Pentecost) celebration of the triumph of life over death, of holiness over sin in the dead and risen Jesus and in us as his disciples. There is an additional festal season in the liturgical year, namely, that of Christmas-Epiphany which is prepared for by Advent. This season has less to do with celebrating the past event of Jesus' birth than is often thought. Yes, we celebrate the birth of the Son of God, but as the basis of the hope which prompts us to look forward to Christ's coming in glory. What we celebrate in these two festal seasons is already contained in each Sunday's eucharist, but in such a compact way that the two festal seasons which unfold the meaning of the paschal mystery of Christ are a welcome aid.

Because the gospel reading is the controlling reading and the eucharist is the celebration of the mystery of Christ, the decision was made to establish a semi-continuous reading of the Synoptic Gospels in a three year cycle for the remaining part of the liturgical year which is called Ordinary Time. Each of the Gospels of Matthew, Mark, and Luke gives us a unique portrait of Jesus so that over a three year period we become familiar with his identity and allow it to shape our identity as the Body of Christ. An interesting aspect of this choice for a semi- continuous reading of the Synoptic Gospels comes to light when we consider that the first suggestion was to select the readings for Ordinary Time to support a systematic presentation of the church's teaching on faith and morals. The Introduction to the Lectionary for Mass tells us why this suggestion was rejected:

> The decision was made . . . not to have an organic harmony of themes designed to aid homiletic instruction. Such an arrangement would be in conflict with the genuine conception of liturgical celebration. The liturgy is always the celebration of the mystery of Christ and makes use of the word of God on the basis of its own tradition, guided not by merely logical or extrinsic concerns but by the desire to proclaim the Gospel and to lead those who believe to the fullness of truth.[2]

In other words, it is the very nature of Christian liturgy which underlies the choice for a semi-continuous reading of the Synoptic Gospels in Ordinary Time. If more attention were paid to this motivation, we would probably not hear the familiar refrain: "The theme of this Sunday's Mass is . . ." Nor would various Sundays in the course of the year be cluttered up with all sorts of causes or themes, such as Vocation Sunday, Communications Sunday, Mission Sunday which have a tendency to obscure the only reason why people assemble on the Day of the Lord. After all, we do not assemble for eucharist to be instructed on a given theme, but to celebrate the mystery of Christ in whom our Christian identity is anchored. The lectionary, therefore, does not have given themes in mind. It deals with God's salvation history which has reached its climax in Jesus Christ. Thanks to the working of the Spirit of the risen Jesus, there is a place for us in this history.

The rationale for the lectionary's Scripture readings is, then, the celebration of the redemptive mystery of Christ, not as past event, but as present actuality. These readings must therefore be understood in function of what the assembled community is, namely, the Body of Christ; and in function of what this assembled community celebrates, namely the paschal mystery of Christ. When proclaimed in the context of the church's worship they evoke the story of Jesus and of salvation history to the point of making the risen Jesus present. Sunday after Sunday we come together around the living Christ so that we who have entered into his death and resurrection by faith and baptism may be grafted into Christ and progressively become what we are called to be: the Body of Christ, the church.

Against this background it should not be difficult to grasp the pattern of readings chosen for the various Sundays. For the two festal seasons, Lent-Easter and Advent-Christmas-Epiphany, an attempt is made to have the readings highlight a particular aspect of the mystery being celebrated. That is why, generally speaking, the Gospel of John has such a prominent place at these times, especially in the Lent-Easter season. The readings fit together well, because the particular season has been the decisive factor in their choice. For the Sundays in Ordinary Time we must keep in mind that the first reading from the Hebrew Scriptures has been chosen in light of the controlling gospel reading. Some serious objections have been raised against this procedure, because it is felt that it does not sufficiently respect the intrinsic value of the Hebrew Scriptures. There is considerable merit in these objections, but, on the other hand, can we as Christians read the Hebrew Scriptures through other than Christian glasses, especially when we celebrate the paschal mystery of Christ? The psalm following the first reading and chosen in light of it almost serves as an additional reading from Scripture. This does not justify its being read; by its very nature it asks to be sung or chanted. The second reading can sometimes present a difficulty because it is a semi-continuous reading of the letters of Paul with no intended relationship to either the gospel or to the first reading. This does not mean, however, that it is always totally unrelated to them.

All in all, we find in the present Sunday lectionary an immensely rich fare of biblical readings. There is no comparison between this and what we had before. Of course, what we have is certainly not the entire Bible. It is more adequately described as a liturgical Bible. In that case, whether the lectionary can function properly will depend on some important liturgical and biblical considerations. From a liturgical perspective, it is presupposed that we understand the eucharist to be the event which effectively makes the paschal mystery of Christ present so that we may enter into it. What is also presupposed is that we appreciate the paschal character of each Sunday and that we are familiar with the rhythm and basic make-up of the liturgical year. From a biblical perspective, the adequate liturgical functioning of the lectionary also presupposes a fair degree of familiarity with the entire Bible. If we lack this familiarity, the Sunday-after-Sunday exposure to considerable portions of it may serve as an incentive to correct this lack. When these liturgical and biblical conditions are met, we can be confident that our sense of who we are as Christians and our weekly celebration of the eucharist will be significantly enhanced.

The Homiletic Moment

The proclamation of the scripture readings in the context of the eucharist is not all there is to the liturgy of the word. This proclamation needs to be complemented by the preaching that immediately follows the readings. Not only should the preaching follow the proclamation of the scripture readings chronologically, its substance should be shaped by them. If the liturgy of the word is to be taken seriously and if preaching is to be seen as an integral part of it, preachers must realize that they are not free to expound on any religious topic that happens to come to mind. Nor is justice done to the integral link of the preaching with the preceding scriptural passages when only scant reference is made to them or when a line or an idea from the readings serves as a pretext for what the preacher was going to say anyway.

What this means is that the worship context in which this preaching takes place must be respected. While most preaching will contain some instructional and catechetical features, instructional or catechetical aims are not to be the focus of preaching within the eucharistic context. People have assembled for worship, for communication with their God. It is understandably tempting to argue "Since they all ought to know this and since they won't come back for sessions of a more educational nature, we'd better preach about it." But this is really a misuse of the worship setting. People have assembled not to be instructed about God or about other important faith matters, but to be led into the mystery of the living God. With all due respect to the need to educate, the eucharist is not the place to do it. We must make sure that we do not deprive the members of the community of those precious moments of "wasting time with their Beloved," of doing "useless things" such as worshiping God and letting themselves be nourished by his word. The preaching moment heightens the intensity of these moments of encounter with God. There is still, among the preachers and the hearers, a considerable unfamiliarity with the sort of preaching that the eucharist demands.

Preaching in the context of the eucharist is more than a matter of giving an interesting talk on a religious topic. The liturgical reform of the last decades says that a homily is what the situation demands. This is not simply a fancy name for what we used to call a sermon. Preaching used to be virtually unrelated to the Mass, even if it occurred during the Mass. The liturgical reform, if it is to be consistent, calls for a different type of preaching. To qualify as a homily, the preaching that follows the scripture readings in the context of the eucharist must meet three criteria: it must be based on Scripture or be biblically centered; it must be relevant to the concerns of the community assembled, that is, it must be directed to the real questions of these people; it must call forth the response of praise and thanksgiving or, in other words, it must be taken up in worship. These criteria were articulated and elaborated by William Skudlarek in his fine book *The Word in Worship*.[3] They have also found their way, in a slightly different form, into the very helpful document from the U.S. National Conference of Bishops, *Fulfilled in Your Hearing*.[4]

It is no coincidence that the preaching takes place after the proclamation of the Scriptures and before the actual eucharist. Its strategic position between these two poles sets the agenda for the preaching. The same scripture readings are proclaimed on a given Sunday all over the globe in all Roman Catholic churches and in many other Christian churches as well. The same Roman Catholic churches will join in giving praise and thanks to God in the eucharistic part of the Mass because of what God has accomplished in the death and resurrection of Jesus for all humanity. They will then share the eucharistic bread and wine. They have done this for centuries and they will continue to do it for centuries to come. These two objective or general elements are, we could say, the two invariables, the two poles between which the homiletic moment is situated.

But each community that places itself before God's word and celebrates the eucharist is unique. Nowhere is there another community which has the unique composition of St. Mark's parish in this place and time. There never was nor will there ever be one exactly like it again. It can be identified as the variable between the two invariables. The preaching moment, at the strategic juncture between the scripture readings and the eucharist is meant to enable this unique and variable parish community to hear God speak his word of salvation. It summons the community to conversion so that it, in turn, can give praise and thanks to God and find a home in the paschal mystery of Christ that is being celebrated in the eucharist. That is, no doubt, a tall order for the preaching moment, but it also shows how extremely important that moment is. Without it the scripture readings might seem to have nothing relevant to say to the unique life experiences of this particular community, and the community might wonder why it should give thanks and praise to God for a redemptive mystery so general and universal that it cannot see how its own life experiences fit within it. The preaching moment must prevent both the proclamation of the word and the celebration of the eucharist from taking place in a vacuum. Their universal significance must be shown to contain salvific meaning for this unique community.

Since its strategic position sets the agenda for the preaching moment, it must complement each of the two poles. Though the biblical readings are normative, they are historically and socially conditioned expressions of the faith experience of diverse communities. The four Gospels, for example, are not timeless divine press releases. Certainly, they find their unity in the once-and-for-all-definitive Jesus-event in which God communicates and reveals himself to us. But the faith response to this offer of salvation in the form of the gospel texts is conditioned by the concrete situations of the different faith communities shaped by that all important Jesus-event. The four Gospels reflect that inevitable diversity because the hope and joy, the struggles and questions of these communities have given these Gospels their form. The faith community of the Christian church has accepted them as authoritative and normative witnesses to the event of salvation from which it draws life. These four Gospels, together with the other canonical writings, have given subsequent generations of Christians access to the event of salvation that lies behind the biblical texts. The wager is that, when we place ourselves as a faith community before this word of God, God will also reveal himself to us as a saving God. Our response in faith to that offer of salvation in Jesus Christ will inevitably be marked by the questions and conditions that are part of our experience of life. It is the task of preaching to provoke this new faith response.

Preachers cannot, therefore, be satisfied with establishing what the biblical text meant originally. They must, of course, be prepared to ascertain that because, even though they may not be professional exegetes, they cannot disregard the findings of biblical studies. But they must also go beyond that. Once they have done their homework, they must use their creative talents to help the assembled community discern the light that the readings are shedding on it so that it may arrive at a unique faith-interpretation of its life experience. In other words, it is not enough to know what the biblical text meant in the past. We still must try to discover what it means now. It has a lot to do with "X-raying" this community's experience of life, with the help of the Scriptures and, through the prism of the biblical witness, detecting God's salvific presence, God's revealing self as a liberating and life-giving God to whom we are summoned to entrust ourselves in order to make sense of life.

With reference to the scripture readings which precede it, the task of preaching, therefore, is to show that the saving activity of God to which they bear witness applies to this community. This should enable its unique situation to be understood, with the eyes of faith, as a new moment, a new page in the history of salvation initiated by God. This means that the homily is more than an explanation of the scriptural text. It may very well be that the biblical texts need to be explained. But our lives are in even greater need of interpretation! They need to be explained with the help of the light that comes from God. The homily's purpose is to provide that. It is meant to be a faith interpretation of the lives of these men and women so that, in the light of Scripture, their own history may be seen to be an instance of salvation history. Homiletic preaching endeavors to make us see our own history as a history addressed by God's word of salvation so that we may know ourselves drawn into the covenant dialogue which the saving God initiates. What it amounts to is that preachers, in the context of the eucharist, are mystagogues. That is to say, they "coach, tease, prod" the hearers into giving themselves over to the God whose identity is revealed in the redemptive mystery that is celebrated.

The preacher's greatest challenge is to mediate and facilitate the community's encounter with the saving intentions of God. The homily is meant to show that this offer of salvation has validity for these hearers so that they may see their life stories as containing moments of grace, in which God reveals himself to them. The homily enables the hearers to read or interpret their lives from a salvific perspective and to see that their existence is being nourished by the substance of the biblical texts. Ideally, what should occur at every homiletic moment is the realization that "this text is being fulfilled today even while you are listening" (Lk 4:21). Preachers will be the first to admit, however, that if this does indeed take place, something is happening that far exceeds their abilities.

But the other pole, the eucharist proper, also makes demands on the preaching moment. The eucharist is the celebration in praise and thanksgiving of the salvation that God offers us in Jesus Christ. The homilist plays a major role in enabling the worshiping assembly to become a praising and thanksgiving community in a realistic way. Salvation in Jesus Christ is celebrated, but the life experience of this community may be such that this salvation is not yet truly visible in its life. There may, in fact, be quite a discrepancy between what is celebrated, namely salvation, and the people's concrete experience of brokenness, or their experience of a mixture of pain and joy, failure and accomplishment, sin and grace, death and life. Christians try to come to terms with this ambiguity by placing it in the perspective of salvation in Christ. It is primarily the homily's task to assist this community to identify with the paschal mystery of Christ. The homily sheds light on the life of

71

these people by placing their experience in the perspective of salvation which is being celebrated. With the help of the scripture readings the community has found a reason to give thanks and praise to God for it has discovered that it can go somewhere with its ambiguity, namely, to the victory of life over death, of sense over nonsense being celebrated here and now in the death and resurrection of Jesus. The life of these people is not left untouched. Rather, it is drawn into the event which we acknowledge as decisive between God and us.

This makes the homily itself a liturgical act and as such integral to the liturgical celebration. What is being witnessed to in the Scriptures and celebrated in the sacrament is made effectively present with the help of the homily which addresses the now of this community. Preachers of homilies are not trying to inform their hearers that salvation has taken place in the past or that it is going to take place in some distant future. They are trying to show that it is taking place now. Therefore, whether the participants are able to locate their lives in what is being celebrated depends very much on the homily. The homily must ensure that what is celebrated is not perceived as something "out there" that has no bearing on the present. The homily is meant to prod and tease these people into identifying with the praise and thanksgiving of the event celebrated because they have encountered the God of salvation in this time and in this place. Ralph Keifer has summed it up very well in his commentary on the Sunday Lectionary *To Hear and Proclaim*: "The task of liturgical preaching . . . becomes one of making a threefold link between biblical story, prayer of the church, and the living experience of the assembly. We come together to celebrate our own grace, to be reconciled with our brokenness, and to find these in the context of the biblical story." The critical questions for homilists to ask are: "'How do we identify Christ in the gospel with Christ in the assembly?'; 'What is the relationship between gospel and eucharistic prayer?' and 'How do they relate to the lives of this assembly of God's people?'"[5]

But we also have to be realistic. The present experience of this community is indeed considered in terms of what has come to light in the Christ event. But this Christ event is not yet complete because we look forward to his coming in glory. That is why this present experience must be placed in a future perspective. Homilists cannot pretend to offer nor can the hearers expect to find a complete answer to the searchings that mark their lives in their present situation. We do indeed celebrate the paschal mystery of Christ in the present, but not as though it is totally accomplished. In fact, built into the present celebration is the promise of the future fulfillment that eludes us in the present. In other words, the actual celebration of the eucharist shares in those questions that underlie the entire Christian faith experience: "God, who are you? Where can you be found?" Part of the Christian faith interpretation of existence is that the complete answer to our searchings cannot be given in this life, because our destiny lies beyond this world. And yet, that future fulfillment influences the present because it empowers us to live in hope. Part of the homilist's task is to help us negotiate a passage through the present situation towards God's future based on what has come to light about that future in the death and resurrection of Jesus which we celebrate in the eucharist. The scripture readings proclaimed in the eucharist speak of what has taken place in the past and what will surely take place in the future. But they do not immediately address the present that is uniquely and inevitably ours. The homily must attempt to do this so that the hearers can get on with life in hope because they feel tuned into God's dream for our world. With the help of the homily, they should be able to situate the more immediate horizon of their experience of life within the ultimate horizon of God's kingdom. They will have to be satisfied, however, with picking up only a trace of it in the present.

Needless to say, the demands placed on the homily are considerable. After all, the issue that is at stake in it is the faith life of the worshipping community. All the more reason for the worshiping community and the homilist to assume their shared responsibility to bring the homily or the homiletic moment out of its isolation. This can be done in different ways. Sharing the responsibility does not mean that just anyone can get up and preach in the church's eucharist. If it meant no more than that, we would still be looking at it as an isolated moment. Our starting point must be that one person in the community which lives from the mystery to which the Bible bears witness is chosen and mandated to speak the word that enables the assembly to find its place in the mystery celebrated. Normally the one who presides over the community's eucharist takes responsibility for this preaching. But that surely ought not to exclude the possibility that, if the community is blessed with the presence of a non-ordained member who apparently has the gift to nourish the faith life of the community, this person be asked to serve the word of God and the community by preaching. But this should not be done at some other time—as is done now in some instances to circumvent a canonical problem—but immediately after the gospel reading. Doing anything else is utterly non-sensical and destroys the basic architecture of the eucharist. To ask whether a lay person can give a homily or not is not a very enlightened question. It is not who speaks after the scripture readings, but what is said that determines whether there is, in fact, a homily.

Apart from that, if the community is prepared to take the homiletic moment more seriously, then it is highly desirable that some mechanism be set up by which the community measures and gauges, to the extent that this is possible, the faith effectiveness of the preaching that occurs in its midst. More is called for than the well-intended and much-appreciated "Good sermon, Father" after Mass. It is a matter of the community claiming ownership of the homiletic moment because its faith is in the balance. It presupposes that both the community as a whole and the homilist within the community see, respect, and support each other as fellow believers and fellow hearers of the word that brings salvation.

The liturgy of the word normally concludes with the general intercessions or the prayers of the faithful. The actual practice shows that we have considerable difficulty with these prayers. They tend to be less expressions and acknowledgments of our standing in need before God than moralizing messages targeted at specific groups of people. This is unfortunate. If the homily has helped us see the saving God at work in our lives and has in some small way encouraged us to entrust ourselves anew to God's salvific intentions, is it not natural that we should want to name some concrete situations and persons that stand in need of God's salvation? Surely, when we are assembled for eucharist we are concerned about more than our own salvation. It is here that we put our baptismal priesthood to work by interceding with God for persons and conditions that rather clearly demonstrate that they are as yet unredeemed and that cry out for God's saving presence. We would not want to close our eyes and our ears to them now that we are about to celebrate God's grace-filled deed of saving the world in the death and resurrection of Jesus. But God does not redeem a world or the human family in general. We would like to think that this salvation is meant for concrete persons and situations in which little of that state of salvation is visible. So we pray.

The reader must have noticed by now that not a word has been said about the creed which is part of our celebration of the eucharist on Sundays. To be honest, the place of the creed in the Sunday eucharist presents a problem. It was introduced into the eucharist as a baptismal feature in the sixth or seventh century when there was a decrease in the appreciation of the eucharistic prayer as the church's profession of faith. So the emphasis on the creed coincided with a loss of appreciation of the eucharistic prayer. Now that the eucharistic reform has led us to begin to appreciate the true function and place of the eucharistic prayer in the context of the church's eucharist, we may begin to see that the creed, in fact, duplicates what is already contained in that prayer. We shall demonstrate this later. The creed really disrupts the basic flow of the eucharist and tends to devalue the eucharistic prayer. That is why it is not included in our reflections which are primarily based on the liturgical shape of the eucharist.

Notes

1. Constitution on the Liturgy 7.

2. Introduction to the Lectionary for Mass 68.

3. William Skudlarek, *The Word in Worship* (Nashville: Abingdon, 1981) 9, 71.

4. The Bishops' Committee on Priestly Life and Ministry, *Fulfilled in Your Hearing: The Homily in the Sunday Assembly* (Washington, D.C.: United States Catholic Conference, 1982).

5. Ralph Keifer, *To Hear and Proclaim* (Washington, D.C.: The National Association of Pastoral Musicians, 1983) 110-111.

CHAPTER SIX

The Liturgy
of the Eucharist

We now turn to the second part of the community's celebration of the eucharist, the liturgy of the eucharist proper. It is especially this part of the eucharist that has been burdened, in the course of the church's history, with significant controversies. The issues of "real presence" and "eucharist as sacrifice" are the most prominent ones. There is often a polemical tone to what is being affirmed about these issues and much of our eucharistic language and practice has been shaped by them. For centuries, these two issues, while actually belonging to the one eucharist, tended to be dealt with separately.

A good example of this virtual separation is provided by the three separate documents which the Council of Trent in the sixteenth century devoted to the eucharist. In 1551 that council issued a document that addressed the concerns raised by the Reformers on the issue of real presence. No less than eleven years later the same council was in a position to present its teaching on the issue of the sacrifice of the Mass to which the Reformers had raised the most serious objections. A few months earlier the Council of Trent had finalized its position on communion because the Reformers had some misgivings concerning the actual practice of this aspect of the eucharist: why did people receive communion so infrequently and, especially, why was the cup withheld from the laity? This is not to suggest that the council invented the separation of these three aspects which are part of the one eucharist. However, by treating the three issues individually the council virtually enshrined the separation of the pertinent issues that had already been part of the church's tradition for some time.

The unfortunate aftermath of these three almost unrelated documents is that after the council the separation of these issues became the normative pattern for eucharistic discourse. What eucharistic theology must do in our time is to reintegrate these three aspects so that we may come to a more integral understanding of the eucharist. I believe that an attempt in this direction can be made when we take the actual liturgical rite of the eucharist as our starting point. If, in the process, we are attentive to the integrity and the uniqueness of the eucharistic prayer, but do not isolate it, we may find a context in which the three aspects which have been almost totally separated can be consistently and coherently situated.

For a proper understanding of what follows, it is imperative that we stay close to what came to light in the chapter on the Last Supper narratives, because they offer a condensed form of the church's understanding of the eucharist. How could it be otherwise since whatever shape the church has given to the eucharist in the course of history has been entirely dependent on what is outlined in these narratives. This has nothing to do with biblical fundamentalism. It is simply a reflection of the church's obligation to be faithful to what its Lord authorizes it to do when it assembles in memory of him.

The Fourfold Action of the Eucharist

The liturgical rite of the eucharist proper contains a significant eucharistic theology. To discover it we must take the basic structure of this part of the eucharist seriously. There are really no surprises here, for the basic structure of the eucharist proper is very simple inasmuch as it follows the Last Supper scene:

| Jesus took bread and cup | — | presentation of bread and wine |

and when he had given thanks	—	eucharistic prayer
he broke the bread	—	breaking of bread
and gave the bread and		
cup to his disciples	—	communion

It is important that we respect the basic dynamic of this fourfold liturgical action and give each part its due weight while keeping in mind its interaction with the others. Two of the four parts, namely the eucharistic prayer and communion, are the high points. They are, however, preceded by significant preparatory gestures: the presentation of the bread and wine and the breaking of the bread. Though these are secondary, they are, nevertheless, indispensable for the flow of this second part of the eucharist. These two gestures have more than functional significance because they, together with the two high points, constitute the eucharist proper. The liturgical reform has made this fourfold action more transparent than it was earlier and, as a result, the reformed rite can serve as an adequate basis for an initial theological reflection on the eucharist.

The Presentation of Bread and Wine

The presentation of bread and wine is a significant gesture. It is not simply something done because we need the bread and wine for communion. Rather, the gesture in all its simplicity evokes a profound truth about ourselves and about our world in the eucharistic context. This is articulated in the brief prayers that accompany the gesture:

Blessed are you, Lord, God of all creation.
Through your goodness we have this bread to offer,
which earth has given and human hands have made.
It will become for us the bread of life.

Blessed are you, Lord, God of all creation.
Through your goodness we have this wine to offer,
fruit of the vine and work of human hands.
It will become our spiritual drink.

At this point in the eucharist the bread and wine embody our human condition standing before God. We bring not simply bread and wine, but ourselves, our world in fact, and we dare to acknowledge our fundamental dependence upon God. For what we present is what we have been given in the first place and, yet, we may claim it as our own. And what we bring also contains what we have made of that which we have been given. The toil and sweat, the pain and joy with which we work are here too. We offer the fruits of the earth, yes, but also the fruit of our labor in the world. In the gesture of presenting bread and wine we express our faith's vision of the meaning of these gifts. But, even more, we express our faith's vision of who we are, our place in the world and what we, who are co-responsible for creation, have made of it. This bread and wine speak not only of our achievements, but also of our failures and our inability to construct a more human world. What we offer is a deeply wounded and broken world, a world that is soiled by our sinfulness. In the gesture of presenting bread and wine the link of the created order with what is soon to be celebrated, namely the paschal mystery of Christ, is safeguarded. But it is a created order that is still badly scarred and infected by human sinfulness. This too is a case of being realistic.

So it is with a vision derived from faith that we present this bread and wine and all that they embody. This vision of faith does more than merely enable us to see and assess the present condition of our existence and of our world. If that were all it did, why would we even bother to acknowledge it or how could we dare face up to it? The vision of faith with which we present the bread and wine also teaches us where to go with this wounded and broken world of ours because faith knows what is to become of our existence and of our world embodied in the bread and wine. This is articulated in "the bread of life" and "our spiritual drink" of the accompanying prayers. In these few words the orientation towards the eucharist becomes more explicit. Our gifts of bread and wine, precisely in the context of the eucharist, will be intercepted, as it were, by the power of the Spirit of the Risen One. When they have been filled with the Spirit they will become the bearers of Christ's salvific presence among us and food and drink for our journey.

They will transform us into Spirit-filled agents of healing and reconciliation for our world.

I am anticipating what is to become of the bread and wine in the eucharistic prayer and what is to become of us when we consume them. After all, the presentation of the bread and wine does not take place in a vacuum. There is a definite and inevitable eucharistic thrust to this gesture which shows that there is a cohesive flow to the fourfold action of the eucharist. We cannot speak of the presentation of bread and wine as though it is something that stands apart from the other eucharistic actions. This gesture expresses the Christian vision that all of creation and all human history find their fulfillment and crowning point in the dead and glorified Christ. It is in this new Adam that human existence finds its true destiny. Our participation in the eucharist in the present gives us a foretaste of this final fulfillment still to come and serves as a pledge that it will ultimately arrive.

The Eucharistic Prayer

It should now be evident that though the eucharistic prayer is the core of the eucharist, it clearly stands in relation to the presentation of the bread and wine, on the one hand, and in relation to our consumption of this bread and wine, on the other. With the eucharistic prayer we are, no doubt, at the heart of the church's celebration of the eucharist. It is a prayer of praise and thanksgiving proclaimed to God over bread and wine which are not left unchanged in the process. In the eucharistic prayer we call upon God to send the Spirit to take hold of the bread and wine and thoroughly transform them so that they may become for us the body and blood of Jesus Christ. When we consume these transformed gifts of bread and wine, we enter into the death and resurrection of Jesus on which our communal identity as the Body of Christ depends and we are nourished by his self-giving. The parallel with the basic structure of the baptismal event is striking. In the baptismal event we give praise and thanks to God over water which the Spirit will imbue with his power so that those who bathe in it may enter into the death and resurrection of Jesus, to use

81

Pauline terms, or be born of God, in the Johannine image. The point is that whether we bathe in water in Jesus' name or whether we share bread and wine in memory of him, these domestic gestures are thoroughly transformed so that they become the vehicles of our entering into that event which we recognize as foundational to our Christian identity.

The claims we make concerning the eucharistic prayer stem, of course, from the uniqueness of this type of prayer. It is a prayer of praise and thanksgiving to God pronounced by the presider on behalf of the community that celebrates the eucharist. But it is a prayer of praise and thanksgiving that proclaims and remembers who God has shown himself to be in creation, in the history of Israel but above all in Jesus Christ, namely a God who liberates, who sets free, who saves us from whatever it is that stands in the way of our living in covenant with God and with each other. It is a prayer that makes God's liberation of humankind in the death and resurrection of Jesus Christ effectively present so that we may enter this all-decisive redemptive event. As such, the prayer is a sequel to what the Scriptures have proclaimed about God's care for us as his people. This sort of remembering and making present is only possible in the power of the Spirit whom the risen Jesus bestows on his church, so that in the midst of all sorts of experiences of non-redemption we may persevere in hope of Christ's coming in glory. The basic core of this prayer of praise and thanksgiving to God is the very reason for which it is uttered, namely God's re-creation of us and our world in Jesus Christ. It is in him that God has laid the foundation for the healing and reconciliation of a wounded and broken humanity. It is in the same Jesus Christ's coming in glory that what God has begun will be brought to completion, when God will bring everything together under Christ as head.

Thus the eucharistic prayer is basically faith's response to what God has done in Jesus Christ and to what he will bring to completion in the power of the Spirit. It is our acknowledgment and proclamation of what we consider to be the key of God's grace-filled dealings with humanity, namely the paschal mystery of Christ which is effectively made present until Christ comes in glory. But until that time we have to be satisfied with participating in it under the veil of signs.

These signs, however, are not empty pointers to the reality for which we give praise and thanks to God; they contain the reality of the body and blood of Christ, the self-giving of Jesus on the basis of which God has established and continues to establish covenant with us and among us. But as bread is to be eaten and wine to be drunk, so in the eucharist the bread and wine which, by the power of the Spirit, have become the body and blood of Christ are also to be eaten and drunk so that we may become the Body of Christ which we consume. The fruit of Christ's self-giving borne by the eucharistized bread and wine is the unity of the Body of Christ, the church. The eucharistic prayers say it in no uncertain terms: "May all of us who share in the body and blood of Christ be brought together in unity by the Holy Spirit" (II), "Grant that we, who are nourished by his body and blood, may be filled with his Holy Spirit, and become one body, one spirit in Christ" (III), "by your Holy Spirit, gather all who share this one bread and one cup into the one body of Christ, a living sacrifice of praise" (IV). It is by the death and resurrection of his Son Jesus that God acquires a holy people for himself. The eucharist has this ecclesial, church-building effect because it is the memorialization of the paschal mystery of Christ from which the church as the Body of Christ derives its identity.

This memorialization includes a so-called eschatological perspective. This is not just a peripheral aspect of the church's eucharist. It is constitutive of it inasmuch as we are given a foretaste of the Messianic Banquet. What we are privileged to celebrate provides the basis for the inevitable forward thrust of the eucharist. The church's celebration of its Lord's Passover as now taking hold in Christ's Body is very similar to the celebration of the Jewish Passover. Just as the latter has a hope-filled looking forward to the full revelation of God's glory built into it, so the church's eucharist is unrecognizable if it does not make us hunger and thirst for the full manifestation of God's Messiah in all his glory. This is, in the final analysis, *the* eucharistic issue. History demonstrates that losing sight of this eschatological perspective inevitably leads to the disastrous results that follow from the emergence of other issues which are said to be *the* eucharistic issues. The recovery of this eschatological thrust, which is so clearly articulated in the eucharistic prayer itself, situates these issues in a creative context so that the coming of God's Kingdom may once more emerge as the dominant preoccupation of the church's eucharist. It is not a matter of introducing a new element but of doing justice to what, in fact, the church professes in the latter part of the eucharistic prayer.

This also applies to the doxology with which the eucharistic prayer concludes. Lest we should forget that the eucharistic prayer is the church's prayer of praise and thanksgiving to God, the closing line sums it all up. The honor and glory of the Father pervades the entire prayer and it is to this that we consent in the concluding Amen. That Amen is more than a verbal consent. In fact, we will underline it ritually by consuming the bread and wine over which the prayer of praise and thanksgiving has been proclaimed. This is to say that we who are privileged to feed on this bread and wine, the body and blood of Christ, want our own lives to give honor and glory to God. Naturally, we can never hope to be strong enough to do this ourselves. It is only possible through, with, and in Jesus Christ and in the unity of the Holy Spirit.

The Communion Rite

Earlier I mentioned that the liturgy of the eucharist proper is a fourfold action. We shall deal with the last two elements together. This may seem inconsistent, and in some way it is but keeping them together shows how closely linked they are, and allows us to consider the two additional elements that the church has introduced as part of the communion rite, the Lord's Prayer and the exchange of peace that precede the actual breaking of the bread and communion. It could be argued that the basic pattern of the eucharist would be more transparent if the eucharistic prayer were immediately followed by the breaking of the bread and communion. After all, the entire thrust of the eucharistic prayer is toward these two actions. Certainly considerable caution is called for because, the more elements we place between the eucharistic prayer and the breaking of the bread and communion, the greater the distance between the eucharistic prayer and the actual taking of communion. If there is too much distance, the basic flow of the entire eucharistic action tends to be broken and there is danger that the actual taking of communion will be perceived as a relatively independent rite.

On the other hand, the Lord's Prayer and the gesture of peace as a ritual underlining of the mutual forgiveness that is called for in the Lord's Prayer are entirely appropriate elements of the communion rite. The Our Father immediately follows the eucharistic prayer in which we have given praise and thanks to the Father. We can only do this because the Spirit of the Risen Jesus with whom we are made one cries out "Abba, Father." Moreover, as part of this being made one with Christ we recognize ourselves as brothers and sisters to each other. If this is all part of the eucharistic prayer, no wonder that the latter almost naturally evolves into our prayerful uttering of our Christian identity in the prayer Jesus gave us. This prayer serves as an immediate preparation for what is integral to the eucharistic action, the receiving of communion in which the substance of what we pray for in the Our Father is sealed.

If we keep this in mind, the gesture of exchanging the peace of Christ can be held in check as well. Needless to say, this is a welcome and significant gesture, but at times it is done so elaborately that the basic flow of the eucharistic action is broken, and the actual receiving of communion becomes almost an afterthought. This is why some suggest that the sign of peace be transferred to another place where it would be less disruptive and equally appropriate: "If you are bringing your offering to the altar and there remember that your brother has something against you, leave your offering there before the altar, go and be reconciled with your brother first, and then come back and present your offering" (Mt 5:23-24).

As for the significance of the breaking of the bread, we can immediately appeal to Paul: "The loaf which we break, is it not a sharing in the body of Christ? And as there is one loaf, so we, although there are many of us, are one single body, for we all share in the one loaf" (1 Cor 10:16-17). It is an ecclesial, church-building interpretation of what may seem at first sight to be a rather

85

functional gesture which the General Instruction of the Roman Missal appropriates:

> The action of the breaking of the bread, the simple term for the eucharist in apostolic times, will more clearly bring out the force and meaning of the sign of the unity of all in one bread and of their charity, since the one bread is being distributed among the members of one family.[1]

It is evidently a matter of letting the eucharistic symbol of the one bread which we share speak instead of taking shortcuts in the form of individual hosts. These simply cannot powerfully evoke the ecclesial significance of actually breaking the bread before those present. The breaking of the bread at this point in the liturgy demonstrates that the way some presiders break the bread at the recitation of the institution narrative is a misplaced gesture.

The significance of the actual communion of bread and wine should be evident from what has already been said about the presentation of the bread and wine and about the eucharistic prayer. If communion is an integral element and not an optional one in the eucharistic action, and if we must allow our symbolic actions to speak, it follows that communion of both bread and wine is simply imperative. Too much of what the eucharist is basically all about gets lost when the cup is only occasionally shared. Even if the General Instruction of the Roman Missal allows for communion under one kind only in the light of the tradition, it very well articulates the reason why communion of the cup is a necessity:

> Holy communion has a more complete form as a sign when it is received under both kinds. For in this manner of reception a fuller light shines on the sign of the eucharistic banquet. Moreover there is a clearer expression of that will by which the new and everlasting covenant is ratified in the blood of the Lord and of the relationship of the eucharistic banquet to the eschatological banquet in the Father's kingdom.[2]

If liturgy is indeed a ritual-symbolic way of acting out how it is between God and us on account of Jesus Christ, then it is hard to justify the practice of communion under the form of bread only.

The men and women who assemble for eucharist on the Day of the Lord have their identity as Body of Christ renewed. They are transformed into new men and women and empowered to share in Christ's continuing mission to reconcile and heal a broken and wounded world. This mission will only be accomplished when we are gathered together at the messianic banquet of which the eucharist is both a foretaste and a pledge.

The Eucharistic Prayer

The eucharistic prayer has already been dealt with in the previous section as part of the fourfold action of the liturgy of the eucharist proper. However, because of its importance and because all aspects of it could not be adequately exposed in the more global setting of the liturgy of the eucharist, it will be worth our while to spend more time on it. Moreover, we have to keep in mind that, for centuries, this prayer was virtually unknown territory for those who attended Mass for the simple reason that it was considered to be an exclusively priestly prayer. The only part that the assembled community was somewhat familiar with was what came to be known as the words of consecration. In addition, the prayer was said in Latin in a low voice, if not in total silence. During the last twenty-five years or so it has been said out loud in English and the celebrating community actively participates in it by acclamations. Furthermore, the roughly fourteen-centuries long monopoly of the Roman Canon has been broken by the introduction of eight other officially approved eucharistic prayers. But these are only the more immediately noticeable changes. The potential it possesses to shape our understanding of the eucharist still remains largely untapped. The beauty of it is that, if we pay close attention to its uniqueness and integrity, aspects of the eucharist come to the fore that have long lain dormant. But its significance is not exhausted by what the eucharistic prayer says about the eucharist itself. It will also become evident that it serves as a comprehensive summation of the Christian faith and even contains a basic outline of the Christian life.

One Corporate Prayer

To make sure that we all know what unit of the entire eucharist we are talking about when dealing with the eucharistic prayer, let me briefly indicate where it begins and where it ends. It begins with the introductory dialogue between presider and congregation after the gifts of bread and wine have been prepared and presented:

> The Lord be with you.
> And also with you.
> Lift up your hearts.
> We lift them up to the Lord.
> Let us give thanks to the Lord our God.
> It is right to give him thanks and praise.

The prayer ends with the great Amen that follows the so-called doxology in which the presider sums up the basic thrust of the entire eucharistic prayer:

> Through him, with him, in him, in the unity of the Holy Spirit, all glory and honor is yours, almighty Father, for ever and ever.

The Amen that follows is the single most important Amen of the community's celebration of the eucharist.

I have indicated the beginning and end of the eucharistic prayer not simply to delineate which section of the eucharist we are dealing with but to demonstrate that even though this prayer is proclaimed by the presider, it is a corporate prayer of the assembled community. We should not conclude from this that all present should say this prayer in unison. This erroneous conclusion does not respect the basic principle that this assembled community is a structured community in which various ministries, including the ministry of presiding, must be given their due weight. The fact that the presiding minister proclaims it does not keep it from being a corporate prayer. The introductory dialogue and the concluding Amen, together with the Holy, holy, holy, the memorial acclamations, and some other acclamations, bring this home.

It is by means of the introductory dialogue that the presider seeks permission and authorization from the community to speak in its name to God. The presider needs to know that the words that are going to be said do indeed express the sentiments of this community. It is a way of making sure that the presider and the community are operating on the same wavelength. The presider articulates the faith, praise, and thanksgiving not only of this local community but of all the eucharistic communities with which this assembly lives in communion.

The concluding Amen also proclaims that the eucharistic prayer is indeed the prayer of the community. "So be it," "Yes, we heartily agree" is what the community proclaims. In this Amen it expresses its agreement with what the presider has proclaimed and articulated on its behalf. In that Amen the community says that it wants to be, in its very life as a eucharistic community, all glory and honor to God, which it can only be through, with and in Christ, in the unity of the Holy Spirit. That is how high the stakes are in this Amen. Consequently, a simple murmuring of this Amen will not do.

But there is an additional reason why we have to be clear on where the eucharistic prayer begins and ends. Not only is it a communal prayer, it is also *one* prayer. Why make this point? The adage "we cannot see the forest for the trees" often applies to the way we look at the eucharistic prayer. Before attending to it in its entirety we have a tendency to split it up into various parts: preface, sanctus, consecration, institution narrative, memorial, epiclesis, doxology. While this approach has some legitimacy, we are in danger of losing sight of the thrust of the entire eucharistic prayer. History provides us with sufficient evidence to prove that we get into serious trouble when we isolate one of the parts and give it so much prominence that we no longer see that it functions properly only when it is part of the whole. This is true of the entire eucharist, but it especially applies to the eucharistic prayer. If we isolate one part, we not only lessen the intelligibility of the eucharistic prayer itself but also of the part we isolate. We may even seriously distort the real meaning of both. If, on the other hand, we respect the integrity of the eucharistic prayer and see the different sections as parts interacting to constitute one composite whole, then we are bound to discover an immense wealth.

The unity and cohesiveness of the eucharistic prayer as well as its corporateness dictate that the assembled community adopt a physical posture that is commensurate with the unique character of this prayer. The standing position is the most appropriate one for the entire eucharistic prayer, because as a community we address God in praise and thanksgiving. It is understandable that, because of certain developments in the past, kneeling was (and in some places still is) the preferred posture especially during the so-called words of consecration. But, from a liturgical perspective, kneeling is appropriate for a penitential disposition which certainly does not apply when we express our praise and thanksgiving as is the case in the eucharistic prayer. Moreover, let us not forget that this posture of kneeling emerged precisely at the time when the eucharistic prayer was considered the prayer of the priest alone and when we had very little sense of its cohesive unity. However understandable kneeling at the words of consecration was in that context, it does not make the entire dynamic of the eucharistic prayer very intelligible. In fact, it militates against it. The very nature of the eucharistic prayer dictates another posture.

The Eucharistic Prayer as the Church's Profession of Faith

One of the principal characteristics of the eucharistic prayer is that in it the church authoritatively utters its eucharistic faith. If we want to know what the church believes the eucharist is all about, then we may safely have recourse to the eucharistic prayer. Any theology and catechesis on the eucharist that takes its inspiration from the eucharistic prayer will be well served by it and be far more cohesive than a theology and catechesis that relies on other starting points. But not only will such a theology and catechesis be more correct eucharistically, it will soon become evident that, when dealing with the eucharist, we are in fact dealing with the basic tenets of the Christian faith itself. This is not surprising, when we consider how central the church's celebration of the eucharist is to its life as a faith community.

If we start from the inner coherence of the entire eucharistic prayer, we shall find in it a profession of faith that easily matches the structure, beauty, contents, and weight of either the Nicene or Apostles' Creed. Note the beautiful parallel between the eucharistic prayer and the church's creed:

Eucharistic Prayer IV	The Creed
Father in heaven, it is right that we should give you thanks and glory	I believe in God the Father...
Father, you so loved the world that in the fullness of time you sent your only Son to be our Savior	I believe in Jesus Christ...
Father, may this Holy Spirit sanctify these offerings	I believe in the Holy Spirit...
Lord, by your Holy Spirit, gather all who share this bread and wine into the one body of Christ	the holy catholic church...
Father, in your mercy grant also to us, your children, to enter into our heavenly inheritance	the resurrection of the body and the life everlasting.

In this case it is important to recognize the difference between the first three elements and the latter two, however much they belong together. Faith in God, Father, Son, and Spirit are the object and the principle of our faith, while our being church and our having the seed of the resurrection in us are engendered by the Spirit dwelling in us. In other words, the last two elements are very much the work of the Spirit. But when we take the five points together we have a clear indication that both the eucharistic prayer and the creed present us with the most authoritative summing up and outline of the Christian faith. But they also give us a rudimentary outline of the Christian life. Whatever our views of what constitutes the Christian life, no Christian would argue about its constitutive features being trinitarian, ecclesial, and eschatological. These may sound like heavy words, but what they spell out is simple:

The Christian life is trinitarian: **Faith**
   • As Christians we are privileged to share in the intimate life of the Trinity:
      — we know ourselves to be sons and daughters of God;
      — in faith and baptism we have been grafted onto Jesus Christ. He is the vine, we are the branches;
      — the life-giving Spirit dwells in us.

The Christian life is ecclesial: **Charity**
   • The above elements make us the Body of Christ, the church, in which we are brothers and sisters to each other. None of us is a believer all by him/herself.

The Christian life is eschatological: **Hope**
   • All that we are as Christians still waits to be brought to completion when Christ comes in glory and we are fully raised to life in him.

Even the theological virtues of faith, hope, and charity find a place here. When we align these basic characteristics of the Christian life with the eucharistic prayer and the creed, the parallel is obvious:

Eucharistic Prayer IV	The Creed	The Christian Life
Father in heaven, it is right that we should give you thanks and glory	I believe in God the Father...	We are sons and daughters of God
Father, you so loved the world that in the fullness of time you sent your only Son to be our Saviour	I believe in Jesus Christ...	We enter the Paschal Mystery of Christ

Father, may this Holy Spirit, sanctify these offerings	I believe in the Holy Spirit..	We are filled with the Spirit
Lord, by your Holy Spirit, gather all who share this bread and wine into the one body of Christ	the holy catholic church...	We are members of the Body of Christ
Father, in your mercy grant also to us, your children, to enter into our heavenly inheritance	the resurrection of the body and the life everlasting	We live in hope of future glory

What conclusion may we draw from this? It is no exaggeration to suggest that the eucharistic prayer, the creed and the Christian life virtually coincide. If that is so, then the eucharistic prayer indeed deserves our attention. The more familiar we become with it, the more cohesion it will bring to a good number of aspects of the Christian faith that frequently seem fragmented and disparate.

Its Structure and Its Themes

Because the eucharistic prayer sometimes feels rather long, it might be helpful to draw attention to its basic structure. This is even more important when we consider that in our church we have nine officially approved eucharistic prayers to choose from: Eucharistic Prayers I-IV, which are the most widely used; three Eucharistic Prayers for Masses with children, and two Eucharistic Prayers for Masses of reconciliation. Being able to make use of no less than nine eucharistic prayers is a real novelty. Until 1969 the only eucharistic prayer in use over the centuries was the so-called Roman Canon which is now Eucharistic Prayer I. It is quite something to realize that the same eucharistic faith can be expressed adequately and authoritatively in nine different ways. It is a clear indication that the eucharist is too overwhelmingly rich to expect that it can be celebrated with only one eucharistic prayer.

However, this does not mean that we are at liberty to express the one eucharistic faith in any form we like. The great variety of eucharistic prayers focused on given themes which appeared in the late 1960s and 1970s do not reflect in most instances the unique characteristics of the eucharistic prayer. They may be inspiring as prayers, but you cannot always recognize the eucharist in them, even though they include the institution narrative. Every eucharistic prayer must respect and adhere to a basic pattern of thanksgiving and intercession. Why? Because of the uniqueness of the Christian faith. The basic structure of the eucharistic prayer brings to light the unique genius of the Hebrew and Christian way of praying which reflects our understanding of God and how God and humanity interrelate.

Christians gratefully acknowledge what a gracious God has done and continues to do for the sake of humanity. We praise and thank God for creation. We praise and thank God for the covenant he made with Israel and to which he forever remains faithful. We praise and thank God for what, above all, he has accomplished for all humanity in the life, death and resurrection of Jesus, and in the outpouring of the Holy Spirit: a broken and wounded humanity has been reconciled and healed in Jesus the Christ, the first born of a re-created humanity.

But this reconciliation and healing of humanity is far from finished. So the community, the church that draws life from what God has already accomplished in the life, death, and resurrection of Jesus intercedes with God. It pleads with God that what he has begun in Jesus may have its desired effect on the community itself and on the entire human family so that all may be reconciled and healed in Jesus Christ. That for which we give thanks still awaits its full effect. The interceding we do here is of a more general nature than the interceding that takes place in the prayers of the faithful after the homily. In the latter our intercession is specific and concrete in light of the needs of actual persons and situations.

Thanksgiving and intercession thus represent the basic structure of the eucharistic prayer. Within this twofold structure we also detect five basic themes. We referred to them when we drew attention to the parallel between the eucharistic prayer, the creed and the outline of the Christian life. We identified them as trinitarian, ecclesial, and eschatological and noted that they sum up the uniqueness of the Christian faith. This particular feature of the eucharistic prayer has remarkable ecumenical implications and possibilities. In 1982 the Faith and Order Commission of the World Council of Churches released its Lima Document, *Baptism, Eucharist and Ministry*. In the section on the meaning of the eucharist it states: "Although the eucharist is essentially one complete act, it will be considered here under the following aspects:

Thanksgiving to the Father
Memorial (Anamnesis) of Christ
Invocation of the Spirit
Communion of the Faithful
Meal of the Kingdom."[3]

These five aspects or themes are not randomly thrown together. They are a condensed expression of the Christian faith which provide one more indication that the eucharistic prayer is really the church's creed in a different key. On the basis of the five aspects we can see that the eucharistic prayer is the church's prayer of praise and thanksgiving addressed to the Father. The reason for our praise and thanksgiving is the life, death, and resurrection of Jesus, the paschal mystery of Christ. In the power of the Spirit we give thanks and remember the all important paschal mystery of Christ in such a way that it becomes effectively present among us. We do this thanking and remembering over bread and wine which, in the power of the Spirit, become the body and blood of Christ. When we share this bread and wine we are, again in the power of the Holy Spirit, privileged to enter into the paschal mystery of Christ, to be made one with and in Christ so that we become the Body of Christ. This gives us a foretaste of the heavenly banquet to which God calls all humanity.

When we align the five aspects which the Lima Document identifies as belonging to the eucharist with the eucharistic prayer and the creed, the parallel is obvious:

Eucharistic Prayer IV	The Creed	The BEM Document
Father in heaven, it is right that we should give you thanks and glory	I believe in God the Father...	Thanksgiving to the Father

Father, you so loved the world that in the fullness of time you sent your only Son to be our Saviour	I believe in Jesus Christ...	Memorial (Anamnesis) of Christ
Father, may this Holy Spirit sanctify these offerings	I believe in the Holy Spirit...	Invocation of the Spirit
Lord, by your Holy Spirit, gather all who share this bread and wine into the one body of Christ	the holy catholic church...	Communion of the Faithful
Father, in your mercy grant also to us, your children, to enter into our heavenly everlasting inheritance	the resurrection of the body and the life	Meal of the Kingdom

How much more evidence do we need before we are convinced that a consistent eucharistic reform has far-reaching ecumenical possibilities? The eucharistic reform in our own church and the eucharist section of the ecumenical Lima Document draw heavily upon the eucharistic liturgies of the earlier centuries when the controversial issues of "the Mass as sacrifice" and "the real presence" had not yet emerged. Does this not suggest that a reconciliation on these issues is within reach? We now have a setting in which the eucharistic controversies of the past can be dealt with anew and possibly even transcended. We must not forget that these controversies arose, in great part, because certain legitimate aspects of the eucharist were isolated from a more comprehensive view of the eucharistic prayer. That is why it is important not to single out and stall, as it were, on one isolated aspect of the eucharist. That inevitably gets us into trouble. We have to stay in tune with the basic dynamic of the eucharistic prayer. When we do that, we begin to find in the eucharistic prayer itself the church's most authoritative profession of what it believes the eucharist to be.

But Where Is the Consecration in All This?

I mentioned that it is crucial when we focus on certain sections of the eucharistic prayer not to lose sight of the comprehensive nature of this prayer. Each part of it functions properly only in interaction with the other parts. No single part of it can be isolated or given such importance that it draws all attention to itself and overshadows the rest of the eucharistic prayer. But this has, in fact, happened in regard to the institution narrative or, as it is popularly called, the words of consecration. It is not that long ago that, when the priest arrived at this point in the eucharistic prayer, bells were rung and the entire church became silent. All this underscored the extreme importance of this moment, for at this point of the Mass the bread and wine were consecrated and transformed into the body and blood of Christ.

I do not mention this to call the consecration of the bread and wine into the body and blood of Christ into question. This is a given of the eucharist to which I wholeheartedly subscribe. But I mention it because the great emphasis placed on the words and the *moment* of consecration tends to act as a hindrance to our attempt to appreciate the basic flow of the *entire* eucharistic prayer. What is more, it also tends to make us overlook some other equally important aspects articulated in the eucharistic prayer. No one, of course, willfully ignores or denies these other aspects; but some people give the consecration of the bread and wine so much importance that little room is left for aspects that are also very much part of the church's eucharistic faith.

Strange as the question may sound, we might ask ourselves whether we really give full weight to the extreme importance of the consecration itself when we put the emphasis on the consecration of the bread and wine? It would be difficult to maintain that the principal purpose of the eucharist is to effect or produce consecrated bread and wine. A real appreciation of the consecration of the bread and wine is gained from setting the consecrated elements of bread and wine in their proper context.

When we speak of something as consecrated, do we not have to speak, first of all, of Jesus Christ as *the Consecrated One*? He is for us the Holy One of God. Whatever consecration we ascribe in the eucharist to the bread and wine must surely be seen in relation to the Consecrated One, Jesus Christ whose life, death, and resurrection is made effectively present in the celebration of the eucharist. The consecrated bread and wine embody and become the bearers of the self-giving of Jesus lived out concretely in obedience to the Father and in life-giving service to others.

If the first term of reference for the consecrated bread and wine is the Consecrated One, Jesus Christ, then the second term of reference is the baptized men and women who have been made into a spiritual house, a holy priesthood, a consecrated nation. Yes, when we speak of consecration we must not forget that on account of our baptism in Jesus' name we have become consecrated men and women. That, in the final analysis, is our baptismal dignity.

In order to do justice to the basic dynamic of the entire eucharistic action it is important to see that the consecration of the bread and wine is closely related to us as consecrated men and women. The bread and wine of the eucharist are not consecrated for their own sake. They are consecrated so that we who are privileged to feed on this consecrated bread and wine, the body and blood of Christ, may become progressively more consecrated. In this consecrated bread and wine we find the Spirit-effected means that nourish and strengthen our being consecrated, our being the Body of Christ. The fourth eucharistic prayer expresses it unambiguously: "Lord, gather all who share this bread and wine into the one body of Christ, a living sacrifice of praise." Yes, the consecration of the bread and wine is very important and it constitutes the eucharist—but not in isolation.

The mystery of the eucharist, after all, has to do with the relationship between Jesus Christ and ourselves. In the life, death, and resurrection of Jesus Christ, in the paschal mystery of Christ, a gracious God has initiated a re-creation of all humanity. It is a re-creation that we are drawn into or that we give ourselves over to in faith and baptism. It is the mystical union between Jesus Christ and ourselves which needs to be sustained and nourished, and this is what happens in fact when we share the body and blood of Christ in the eucharist. The bread and wine are consecrated for our sake. There are a few lines by the fifth-century bishop Saint Augustine which speak of this eucharistic mystery in a most profound way:

If you are the Body of Christ and His members, your mystery has been placed on the Lord's table, you receive your mystery. You reply "Amen" to that which you are, and by replying you consent. For you hear "the Body of Christ," and you reply "Amen." Be a member of Christ so that your "Amen" may be true."[4]

If we respect the basic flow of the eucharistic prayer, it is obvious that we miss a great deal when we focus almost exclusively on what happens to the bread and wine. We cannot stall on the consecrated bread and wine for the simple reason that in his self-giving Jesus does not have consecrated bread and wine in mind. He is thinking of us. The risen Jesus, the New Adam, wants to change us, to make us into new men and women.

Notes

1. General Instruction of the Roman Missal 283.
2. Ibid. 240.
3. "Eucharist" section of *Baptism, Eucharist and Ministry* (Geneva: World Council of Churches, 1982) 2.
4. St. Augustine, *Sermo* 272.

CHAPTER SEVEN

A Different Context for "The" Eucharistic Issues

One of the difficulties with the orientation of eucharistic theology since the second millennium is that it developed with little reference to the actual liturgy of the eucharist. Doctrinal concern was more prominent than liturgical anchorage. There were considerable gains but in taking this approach eucharistic theology ran the risk of developing refined theological positions which hindered an authentic eucharistic liturgy. The dangers of this trend are evident in the emphasis on the "real presence" and the "sacrifice of the Mass" as the most important issues in eucharistic theology. The theological sophistry which marked this era did not provide good eucharistic liturgy.

We cannot, of course, go over these issues in detail. On the other hand, they still have such a grip on Roman Catholic eucharistic consciousness that it would be unrealistic to simply ignore them. But if we hold to the actual eucharistic liturgy and, especially, the eucharistic prayer as a primary source of theological reflection on the eucharist, it may help to point out that when these issues are taken out of isolation they can be situated within a much more productive context.

Which Is the Body of Christ?

In the previous section I drew attention to the need to set the consecration of the bread and wine in its proper context. We can legitimately and very fruitfully apply the same broadening of perspective to the issue of the real presence, for, in the course of the church's history, that too has undergone a narrowing of focus with serious repercussions especially on our understanding of eucharist and church. For clarity's sake, we must go back a bit in history and ask where the preoccupation with the real presence came from. What made the Christian tradition speak so emphatically of the consecrated bread as the body of Christ? As with so many other issues, history can be a good teacher on this point.

One thing that must be made clear is that the consecrated bread as the real body of Christ was not a serious issue until certain controversies made it so in the ninth and eleventh centuries. Before that time, and particularly in the first five or six centuries, the dominant eucharistic symbols were not objects, but actions. What does this mean? At the risk of oversimplification it is safe to say that in the earlier centuries eucharistic thinking did not focus on the objects of bread and wine and on what happens to them in the eucharist. In retrospect we could say that they considered other aspects of the eucharist more important, such as assembling, listening to the Scriptures, giving thanks over the bread and wine, and sharing them. They certainly did not handle the eucharistized bread and wine disrespectfully nor did they deal with them as ordinary food and drink. No, they surrounded them with reverence and with great care, just as they handled the Bible, and especially the Book of the Gospels, with reverence and devotion. But because they experienced the eucharist differently, the bread and wine themselves were not the issue.

The different way of experiencing the eucharist can best be illustrated by what the notion "body of Christ" evoked in different epochs. The French theologian Henri de Lubac's research in this area some fifty years ago produced really fascinating results. Although for centuries we have linked the notion "body of Christ" almost exclusively with the consecrated bread, in the first centuries Christians used it in two senses, hardly distinguishable from one another. Body of Christ meant both the ecclesial Body of Christ, that is to say the church, and the eucharistic body of Christ, in the consecrated bread. The assembly was designated the Body of Christ especially when it was doing eucharist.

Although the classification is somewhat artificial, if we were to rank the two, the ecclesial Body of Christ would have priority over the eucharistic body of Christ. After all, the Spirit of the glorified Christ empowers the eucharistic body of Christ to build up and transform those who feed on it into the ecclesial Body of Christ. The consecrated bread becomes the body of Christ in order to build up the church which, by the way, is identified as the real Body of Christ. This explains why the celebration of the eucharist was seen as the sacrament of the unity of the church and why there was little need to concentrate on the consecrated bread. The overriding sense was that the glorified Christ continues to build his real Body, the church, by means of his mystical body, the eucharistic bread. The church-building significance of the eucharist was uppermost. The quote from Saint Augustine mentioned earlier deserves to be repeated, because it expresses the issue so very well:

> If you wish to understand the Body of Christ, listen to the Apostle as he says to the faithful "You are the Body of Christ, and his members" (1 Cor 12:27). If, therefore, you are the Body of Christ and his members, your mystery has been placed on the Lord's table, you receive your mystery. You reply "Amen" to that which you are, and by replying "Amen" to that which you are, and by replying "Amen" you consent. For you hear "The Body of Christ", and you reply "Amen". Be a member of the Body of Christ so that your "Amen" may be true.[1]

But then, ever so slowly, things began to shift. It was not an abrupt decision that made this happen, but a slow, almost imperceptible process which reflects a different approach to the eucharistic reality. The elements of bread and wine, but especially the bread, began to attract more and more attention and became the dominant eucharistic symbols at the expense of the actions of assembling, listening, thanking, and sharing.

As part of this move from action to object some influential theologians in the ninth and eleventh centuries began to wonder and argue about the exact relationship between the glorified Christ in heaven and his presence in the consecrated bread. The question that really preoccupied them was whether the eucharistic body of Christ is really the body of Christ or whether it relates to the glorified Christ in the manner of a sign, in which case it would not be the real body of Christ, at least according to the categories they were using at the time. In other words, they played sign against reality. It had to be one or the other. From the triumph of the real there developed other notions, such as the "real presence under the appearance of bread".

It is very important to be aware of this way of looking at the eucharist at the turn of the first millennium, because this new way of looking at it has marked the church for almost a thousand years. We are still influenced by it. Once the battle over the real was settled, new questions surfaced, questions that Christians in the earlier centuries would never have dreamed of: How does the bread become the body of Christ? Who can bring it about? When does it happen? Neither the questions nor the answers need detain us, but we should at least mention the answers in the sequence of the questions raised: transubstantiation, the priest, and at the words of consecration. For many people these ideas still are part of the typically Roman Catholic eucharistic discourse.

Not only eucharistic theology and language were shaped by this preoccupation with the real presence issue. It also spawned eucharistic practices and devotions that expressed the new way in which the church had begun to approach the eucharist. For example, the bread and cup were elevated at the moment of consecration and this gesture was accompanied by the ringing of bells. Practices such as the adoration of the blessed sacrament developed. Notice in this regard that it is not the eucharistic action in its entirety that is called the sacrament, but the consecrated bread. The tabernacle where the blessed sacrament is kept becomes more prominent. The priest has to have a bigger host which can hardly be recognized as bread, while the lay people, who receive communion less and less, have to be satisfied with smaller hosts. In fact, certain practices developed over the centuries that made communion into a devotional exercise rather than an integral part of the eucharistic action so that communion might be received apart from, before, and even during the Mass. It is no exaggeration to say that these strange emphases and the questionable practices they spawned blurred people's perception of the basic coherence and integrity of the entire eucharistic action. The focus was on what the priest effected and what, as a result of that, could stimulate our eucharistic piety.

The unfortunate side effect of these developments was that the eucharist was no longer perceived as the corporate activity of the community and that the sense of the eucharist building up the Body of Christ faded. This is not simply of historical interest because these same developments express themselves in a more contemporary phenomenon, the so-called communion services to which some parishes have recourse when they assemble on Sunday without a priest. This practice is, I believe, yet another manifestation of these questionable eucharistic developments. However understandable the practice of these parishes is, it is built on the wrong eucharistic premises.

This preoccupation with the consecrated bread as the real body of Christ has a disorienting effect not only on the eucharist itself but on our understanding and appreciation of what church is. Prior to the shift at the first millennium, the community's celebration of the eucharist was central to the notion of church as body of Christ. The eucharistic body of Christ was there only in relation to the ecclesial Body of Christ. But with the emphasis on the relationship between the glorified Christ and the consecrated bread, people lost sight of the link between the eucharistic and the ecclesial Body of Christ, the church. How the first body builds up the second was of little concern, with the result that the church was allowed, as it were, to go off on its own. So a notion of church developed that had lost its eucharistic moorings. It was no longer common to mean by "church" first of all the local community with the celebration of the eucharist as its center. Church came to mean a universal hierarchical institution with the pope as its head. The institutional dimension is, of course, also part of the church, but when this becomes what we mean by "church" what becomes of the church's eucharistic dimension?

The liturgical renewal in our century has tried to bring the two notions of the body of Christ together again. This is not just a theoretical issue. Making the celebration of the eucharist into an activity of the assembled community presided over by the priest will inevitably affect how we understand and experience both the eucharist and the church. The two are inseparable inasmuch as one of the primary purposes of the eucharist is to build up the Body of Christ, the church. When, for example, at communion time the priest or the minister of communion shares with us the consecrated bread with the words "The body of Christ", we do more in our "Amen" than profess our faith in the real presence of Christ in the consecrated bread. Over and above that we, together with the other people who receive communion, consent to being made into the Body of Christ. In other words, it is the church-building significance of the eucharist which comes to the fore when we give the notion "Body of Christ" its due weight.

It is in the celebration of the eucharist that the community is most visibly the Body of Christ. Here is where the church of Christ is constituted in a visible and tangible form, that is to say, in a sacramental form. Of course, there are many such local communities in which the church as the Body of Christ is constituted. For all these communities really to be concrete realizations of the one Body of Christ, they need to be in communion with each other. They need to profess the same apostolic faith and to recognize that fact. This being in communion with each other and this professing the same apostolic faith account for both the catholicity and apostolicity of each local eucharistic community. Each local parish community expresses these dimensions of its faith life which it celebrates in the eucharist by its bond with the local bishop who is the chief pastor and the primary guardian of the catholic and apostolic faith of each eucharistic community. Through its union with the local bishop each local eucharistic community is in communion with the universal church.

A word of caution might be in order here. After all, the recovery of the church-building significance of the eucharist must not make us stop at the church as if this is the end-all of the eucharist. We become the Body of Christ, the church, by means of the eucharist in order to share in the intimate life of the Trinity. Our faith is not an isolated, individualistic faith, but an ecclesial faith, lived, expressed, and nourished in the eucharistic assembly, which has God, Father, Son, and Spirit as its ultimate object and goal. The celebration of the eucharist sustains in us the life of the Trinity which we share by faith and baptism.

This is a dimension of eucharistic theology which we have become more aware of as a result of our dialogue with the Orthodox faith experience. In 1982 the official Orthodox - Roman Catholic International Theological Commission published its first theological consensus statement on the eucharist. It gave this document what seems at first sight a rather unwieldy title: "The Mystery of the Church and of the Eucharist in the Light of the Mystery of the Holy Trinity."[2] In hindsight, we can see that it could not have chosen a more appropriate title to indicate that neither the church nor the eucharist constitute an end in itself. Both serve to give us access to the mystery of the Trinity in which our final destiny lies.

Some may wonder why we should complicate the eucharist by dragging the mystery of the Trinity into it. But far from complicating the eucharist, the Trinity provides the church's eucharistic activity with its ultimate rationale. It is precisely when we divorce the church's eucharist from its trinitarian thrust that it becomes complicated. It is when we attend to the intimate life of the Trinity as the ultimate horizon of the eucharist that we can situate the church's eucharist within the basic dynamic of the history of salvation. It is precisely when we lose sight of this ultimate horizon of both eucharist and church that we become hopelessly and tragically divided. History proves it.

This trinitarian dimension of the eucharist is also the ground for the love and unity that are to be characteristic of the eucharistic community. They are no less than the reflection of the communion of love and life among the three persons of the Blessed Trinity. As the 1982 Orthodox-Roman Catholic document puts it:

> By the communion in the body and blood of Christ, the faithful grow in that mystical divinization which makes them dwell in the Son and the Father, through the Spirit . . . The Spirit puts into communion with the Body of Christ those who share the same bread and the same cup. Starting from there, the church manifests what it is, the sacrament of the Trinitarian *koinonia*, the "dwelling of God with people" (Rev. 21:3)[3]

Lest we look upon this dimension of the eucharist as no more than a lofty thought, we might want to assess our eucharistic practice in light of the imperatives which the Lima Document mentioned earlier articulates in the context of the Eucharist as Communion of the Faithful:

> All kinds of injustice, racism, separation and lack of freedom are radically challenged when we share in the body and blood of Christ. Through the eucharist the all-renewing grace of God penetrates and restores human personality and dignity. The eucharist involves the believer in the central event of the world's history. As participants in the eucharist, therefore, we prove inconsistent if we are not actively participating in this ongoing restoration of the world's situation and the human condition. The eucharist shows us that our behavior is inconsistent in face of the reconciling presence of God in human history: we are placed under continual judgment by the persistence of unjust relationships of all kinds in our society, the manifold divisions on account of human pride, material interest and power politics and, above all, the obstinacy of unjustifiable confessional oppositions within the body of Christ.[4]

It is the Orthodox - Roman Catholic Bilateral Consultation in the United States which has most succinctly articulated the eucharistic issues with which we have been wrestling in this section. It has done so in the context of its 1989 document on "Primacy and Conciliarity" from which I would like to quote one pertinent paragraph:

> When it gathers under the life-giving impulse of the Holy Spirit to celebrate in the eucharist the Son's "obedience unto death" (Phil. 2:8) and to be nourished by participation in his risen life, the church most fully expresses what in God's order of salvation it is: an assembly of faithful human persons who are brought into communion by and with the persons of the Holy Trinity, and who look forward to the fulfillment of that communion in eternal glory. So the clearest human reflection of the church's divine vocation is the Christian community united to celebrate the eucharist, gathered by its common

faith in all its variety of persons and functions around a single table, under a single president (*proestos*), to hear the Gospel proclaimed and to share in the sacramental reality of the Lord's flesh and blood (Ignatius, Eph. 5:2-3; Philad. 4), and so to manifest those gathered there as "partakers of the divine nature" (2 Pt. 1:4). "If you are the body of Christ and his members", proclaims St. Augustine, "your divine mystery is set on the table of the Lord; you receive your own mystery . . . Be what you see and receive what you are" (Serm. 272).[5]

If all this sounds too heavy, deep or intricate, a good solution might be to place ourselves before the immensely powerful icon of the Trinity by the fifteenth-century painter Rublev. This icon expresses the profound mystery of the eucharist better than any other medium other than the actual celebration of the eucharist itself.

The Eucharist as Sacrifice

The application of the term "sacrifice" to the eucharist in such titles as the Sacrifice of the Mass and the practices associated with it has been the most difficult issue in the eucharistic controversies between the Churches of the Reformation and the Roman Catholic Church. But remarkable progress has been made. Even if it is too early to speak of a consensus, there is, nevertheless, a significant convergence that gives grounds for hope. What has made this emerging convergence possible? One of the most important factors is unquestionably the recovery of the integrity of the eucharistic prayer and the introduction of new eucharistic prayers. Of course, these developments did not occur in a vacuum. Biblical studies and research done on the eucharistic liturgies of the earlier centuries have enabled theologians from different churches to make important joint affirmations that provide a new context for the question of the eucharist as sacrifice.

It would be presumptuous to suggest that in a few pages we can resolve all the difficulties that pertain to the issue of the sacrifice of the Mass. On the other hand, in the light of what has been presented, we are in a position to make some observations that we hope will be helpful. This is done not only for ecumenical purposes, but also to show that in Roman Catholic circles the issue is not as fixed or untouchable as is sometimes suggested. The observations made here will focus primarily on the caution that is called for in using the category "sacrifice" and on the need to situate this notion properly when we apply it to the eucharist.

The Caution That Is Called for

We cannot possibly delve into the highly technical studies that have been devoted to the question of the eucharist as sacrifice. For our purposes we shall stay close to the popular understanding of the issue where, without much difficulty, we can discern two rather distinct positions. The members of the one group are quite adamant in maintaining sacrificial language to identify the primary characteristic of the eucharist. They insist that there is simply no other appropriate way of speaking about the eucharist. The adherents of the other group are equally reluctant to use any sort of sacrificial language in reference to the eucharist. They do not know what to do with this language when it is applied to the eucharist. It is no secret that the two groups have difficulty understanding each other.

The difficulty is raised most forcefully in the often repeated question: "Is the eucharist a sacrifice or not?" Quite apart from the polemical tone in which the question tends to be raised, it is not easily answered. Much depends on what is meant by it. When the question is phrased this way, it is usually not so much a question as a statement about the eucharist that cannot be challenged because, in the questioner's mind at least, the answer is self-evident. The fact that the eucharist has been called "the Sacrifice of the Mass" for centuries does not seem to leave much room for speaking about the eucharist in any other way. But when the question is phrased this way, it leaves a fair amount unsaid and it seems to be based on assumptions that we may need to expose, if we are at all interested in knowing whether or not it can be answered satisfactorily.

In strictly theological circles and in the official teaching of the church the designation of the Mass as sacrifice has been upheld with a considerable number of qualifications and nuances. But these nuances have not always found their way into the popular perception about the Mass and, therefore, at the popular level, a less nuanced understanding of the Mass as sacrifice is at work. At the risk of oversimplification let me try to sketch this popular perception which does not hesitate to insist that the Mass is a sacrifice and that this is in fact the only way in which to properly identify the eucharist.

First, the custom of speaking of the Mass as a sacrifice has much to do with the way in which religion—how we relate to God—is understood. A sacrificial system was thought to be an inherent part of every religion. If, then, the Christian religion is the most eminent religion, the argument went, it too must have a sacrifice at its center. The sacrifice of the Mass, because of its relationship to the sacrifice of Jesus, seems to fit this notion of religion very well, because we are dealing with the sacrifice of the God-man Jesus Christ in whom, as in no other, our relationship with God is assured.

Second, what notion of God is behind the question? Is the description of the Mass as a sacrifice perhaps propelled by the idea that, in order to have our relationship with God put right, God needs our sacrifices? Does God seek proportionate restitution for offenses committed? Are sacrifices necessary to obtain God's favor? Does the eucharist fit into that slot? It is very important here to be attentive to what seems to be implied and to ask ourselves whether what seems to be implied is really what we want to say.

Third, speaking of the Mass as sacrifice is, to a very large extent, conditioned by a particular view of Christ's death which is made present in the eucharist in "an unbloody manner." But, without minimizing the salvific significance of Jesus' death, can his death be captured only under the category of sacrifice? Moreover, do we not run the risk of isolating the death of Jesus from the rest of his life and above all from his resurrection? Why this narrow preoccupation with the death of Jesus which had to be underlined, it was felt, by hanging an imposing crucifix above the altar of sacrifice? Does it have anything to do with the notion that, if something is to be a sacrifice, it must be experienced as negative and even painful?

Fourth, historically, the increased prominence given to the notion of sacrifice had a lot to do with a significant shift in eucharistic practices. The Mass went from being the Christian community's weekly celebration of Christ's victory over death and the forces of evil, or the church's anticipation of the meal in the heavenly Kingdom to being the sacrifice which the priest could offer for a variety of purposes, especially to obtain God's forgiveness for the dead. The proliferation of Masses and the number of side altars in churches and chapels are not foreign to this. The question is whether the almost exclusive designation of the Mass as sacrifice and the subsequent legitimation of it by way of dogmatic pronouncements did not come close to justifying popular practices which, while legitimate in some way, have a tendency to obscure the primary significance of the community's eucharist.

Fifth, closely linked to these practices is a certain notion of priesthood. The priest tends to be seen as a cultic figure whose primary task it is to offer the sacrifice of the Mass. In this case the priest is not the one who presides over the faith- and worship-life of the assembled community and who, as such, has a place within the community but someone who alone is empowered to perform a sacred action for the sake of the community or certain persons. The phenomenon of Mass stipends, so very difficult to explain and defend, especially when one considers the practices that emanate from it, is very much part of this perception of the eucharist.

If the mentality represented by these five points is behind the question "Is the eucharist a sacrifice or not?", then we have good reason to hesitate to give a straightforward yes to the question. An understanding of the eucharist that is so exclusively sacrificial—and sacrificial in a very narrow sense, because it is only the death of Jesus that is kept in view—inevitably gives rise to another question because one thing is certain: any eucharistic theology embodies and reflects how we understand God and how we see Jesus Christ function between God and us. The eucharist can simply not be understood apart from the Christ event which is made present in it. So the question is whether the eucharistic understanding and practice outlined above sufficiently respect the uniqueness of the Christian religion which comes to light in the immensely paradoxical mystery of Christ. How can the church-building effect of the eucharist that we looked at in the previous section be accounted for in the type of sacrificial understanding of eucharist we just outlined? Can the church-building effect of the eucharist simply be relegated to the status of a marginal feature in order to hold to a rather narrow understanding of the sacrificial nature of the Mass?

Questions like this make it quite evident that establishing that the eucharist is a sacrifice is not a straightforward issue. What are the implications? Prior to determining whether or not the Mass is a sacrifice, we must ask whether the death of Jesus is most aptly understood in sacrificial terms and whether this is the only way it can be interpreted. It is indeed true that in some biblical passages and in the tradition of the church the salvific significance of the death of Jesus has been captured in the category of sacrifice. But when the notion of sacrifice is applied to the death of Jesus something very significant happens to it, particularly to the way it functions in our relationship with God. If it is true that the popular notion of sacrifice evokes the idea that we offer something to God in order to gain God's favor, then we must realize that this is no longer applicable in the Christian dispensation.

In Jesus something entirely new is on the scene and it overturns our hope of putting our relationship with God right by means of sacrificial offerings. What we hope to achieve is indeed accomplished, but by means utterly different than our sacrifices. I am reminded of David Power's reflection on the Suffering Servant theme which is so crucial to understanding Jesus and, consequently, the eucharist:

> He is an innocent person, sent to the people by Yahweh as his messenger, and though persecuted and reviled by them he is obedient, compassionate, uncomplaining in his death. He achieves all that sacrifice cannot, with its attempts at substitution, its shedding of blood and its making of offerings. Indeed, the advent of such a figure on the scene of history renders sacrifices unnecessary, if not actually obscene. The schema of justice which prevails in the making of sacrificial offerings is replaced by the schema of compassion, which witnesses to love and mercy. Expiation is brought about, not by the offerings of the people, but through the witness given in the sufferings and death of the servant, on account of which God manifests him in glory in the eyes of the Gentile nations.[6]

113

The bonding between God and ourselves, for which people offer sacrifices in order to bring it about, has been accomplished in an unheard of fashion. The sacrifices people used to make must give way to this utterly new mode.

This new mode which is the self-giving of Jesus in obedience to God and in life-giving service to us characterizes his entire life and culminates in his death on the cross. It is a self-giving unto the end which, in the final analysis, embodies God's love for us. The Father's raising Jesus from the dead for our sake seals for ever the covenant between God and us. In Jesus God gives to us, not we to God. In Jesus God reaches out to us and heals a wounded humanity. The question we must be willing to ask is whether, in the designation of the Mass as sacrifice and in the practices that follow from this conception, the newness and uniqueness of the mystery of Christ are safeguarded.

The Eucharist as Sacrifice of Praise and Thanksgiving

Nothing of this newness and uniqueness of the mystery of Christ is lost, when as church we are privileged, in the power of the Spirit, to make this mystery of Christ present among us in the celebration of the eucharist. But if the primary characteristic of the self-giving of Jesus accepted by the Father is the accomplishment by God of what no human sacrifices could accomplish, namely communion between God and us, then this will inevitably color the church's celebration of the eucharist as well. Nothing in the celebration of the eucharist can in the slightest suggest that we can put back in place what the self-giving of Jesus has overturned. The celebration of the eucharist can only be the church's acknowledgment and acceptance in praise and thanksgiving of what God offers us in Jesus. There are few places where this point has been made with greater forcefulness than in the following somewhat lengthy quotation from Enrico Mazza:

> Given the impossibility of a true exchange of gifts, human beings can offer only their thanks. This is the sole gift that can be given to the giver who is God. By our praise and thanksgiving, we confess the greatness of his work and his gift. In the

Eucharist, we reach the high point of the order of gifts, and we even pass beyond that order, since our gratitude, the gift we offer to God in exchange, does not represent an exchange in the true and proper sense. In fact, gratitude is simply the way of receiving and accepting a gift. We even pass beyond the order of giving, because here there is no return of an authentic gift on our part (such a return is simply impossible for us, since all we have has been received). Yet we do not leave behind the logic of the "system of gifts" since our response or "return", namely our thanksgiving, is defined as "truly right and just, and our duty." In this passage to the Eucharist, the "system of gifts" loses its content, since no true exchange of gifts is possible with God, but the form of the system is retained because gratitude, which is our way of accepting God's gift, becomes a hymn of praise and thanksgiving that rises to God and is formally offered to him.[7]

This is precisely what the eucharistic prayer is: "a hymn of praise and thanksgiving that rises to God and is formally offered to him." If we offer anything in the eucharist, it is first and foremost this prayer of praise and thanksgiving to God that the Spirit dwelling in us individually and communally prompts us to make. Here is where the Spirit-filled Body of Christ, the assembled community gives voice to its heart in a prayer of praise and thanksgiving that proclaims the great deed of God's love and compassion embodied in the life, death, and resurrection of Jesus Christ. But this proclamation of the paschal mystery makes this mystery effectively present among us. It is an anamnetic proclamation, a proclamation that remembers in a typically Judeo-Christian way, a thanksgiving followed by the church's intercession in the hope that God's deed of love and compassion in Jesus may have its desired effect on our wounded and disjointed world until Christ comes in full glory.

We are confronted once again by the basic elements that constitute the church's eucharist. They come to light as a result of the recovery of the integrity of the eucharistic prayer in the context of the liturgy. Does giving the eucharistic prayer its due weight deny that the eucharist is a sacrifice? Hardly. It does, however, bring the unique way in which God, through the Christ-event, has redefined humanity's way of relating to him into sharper focus. In the celebration of the eucharist the Christian community never ceases thanking God for this and praying that this redefinition will never cease to have its desired effect on our world.

It follows from this that we should be a bit cautious about the popular notion that the primary reason for celebrating the eucharist is so that it can be offered for a variety of causes. Noble though these causes may be, they hardly justify, as the popular expression has it, "having a Mass said." These various causes are more appropriately dealt with in the restored general intercessions of the prayers of the faithful. It is perhaps symptomatic that the Mass began to be used for all sorts of purposes when the prayers of the faithful disappeared from the eucharist and when the Mass became the almost exclusive property of the priest who, moreover, was asked to act as a cultic figure. When these various intentions are once again given a place in the prayers of the faithful and the eucharist becomes the corporate act of the eucharistic assembly, it is freed from the need to serve purposes that tend to be too narrow. It once again becomes the source from which the Christian community can draw strength and hope.

What we are arguing for here is really nothing new. It flows from what the faith community professes and proclaims in the rediscovered eucharistic prayer. When the faith community assembles on the Day of the Lord, it is once again brought in touch with its very roots and is empowered for its mission. As men and women who have been incorporated into Christ in baptism and transformed by the Spirit, in the celebration of the eucharist, we are drawn into Jesus' self-giving. It is from this perspective that the eucharist can be understood as the self-giving of the church. This must not be understood as though the church can offer something apart from Jesus Christ or that the church can offer Christ to God. When the church as the community of baptized men and women celebrates the eucharist, the self-giving of Jesus that is celebrated includes the self-giving of those who have been privileged to enter into the mystery of Christ their Lord who is the head of the Body of which they are the members.

Their living from and their entering into that self-giving of Jesus becomes concrete in the sharing of the eucharistic bread and wine which in sacramental form contain the self-giving of Jesus. After all, this is part of what is unique about the consuming of this eucharistic bread and wine. Every other consuming of bread and wine changes the bread and wine into those who eat and drink; but this consuming of the body and blood of Christ changes us into what we consume, as Saint Augustine noted. It is then through, with, and in Jesus Christ and in the power of the Holy Spirit that the lives of those who engage in the church's eucharistic activity become a living sacrifice of praise to God and a life-giving service to the world. Celebrating the eucharist in that light is an activity that cannot be taken lightly. In this case we do well to realize that the real worship of God to which Christians are summoned does not take place in a beautiful liturgical celebration in the church building but in life itself. This does not invalidate the formal celebration of the eucharist. It only highlights that, if such a celebration is to be authentic, it must encompass all of life.

There is no question that a rediscovery of the importance and centrality of the eucharistic prayer sheds new light on the notion of the eucharist as sacrifice. This does not impoverish the eucharist. Instead, it emphasizes aspects that have been neglected for too long. Paying attention to them can only enrich the church's celebration of the eucharist.

Notes

1. St. Augustine, *Sermo* 272.

2. Joint Commission for Theological Dialogue between the Roman Catholic Church and the Orthodox Church, "The Mystery of the Church and of the Eucharist in the Light of the Mystery of the Holy Trinity," in *Origins* 12 (1982) 157-160.

3. Ibid. no. 4d.

4. "Eucharist" section of *Baptism, Eucharist and Ministry* (Geneva: World Council of Churches, 1982) no. 20.

5. Orthodox-Roman Catholic Bilateral Consultation in the United States, "Primacy and Conciliarity," in *Origins* 19 (1989) 471, no. 3.

6. David Power, "Words That Crack: The Uses of 'Sacrifice' in Eucharistic Discourse," in Kevin Seasoltz, ed., *Living Bread, Saving Cup* (Collegeville: The Liturgical Press, 1982) 162-163.

7. Enrico Mazza, *The Eucharistic Prayers of the Roman Rite* (New York: Pueblo Publishing Co., 1986) 46.

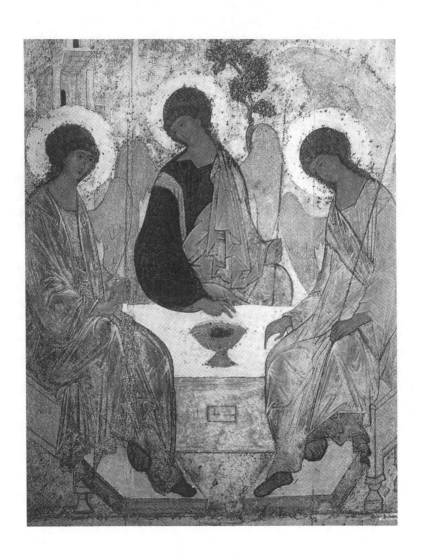

Epilogue

On Trinity Sunday it was my turn to preside and preach at the celebration of the eucharist of the parish community with which I am associated. Preaching on such a Sunday is quite a challenge. I am fortunate to be the owner of a rather large reproduction of Rublev's icon of the Blessed Trinity. I placed the icon at a prominent place in the church so that all assembled could see it in the hope that those assembled might get a taste of what it means to dwell in the house of love, life, and tenderness to which this icon invites us. At least one of the principal purposes for which Rublev painted the icon is, as Henry Nouwen suggests,[1] to keep our hearts centered in God while living in the midst of a world marked by fear, hatred, violence, unrest, and death. The icon serves as a gentle invitation to participate in the intimate communion of love, life, and tenderness that is so characteristic of the way the three divine persons relate to each other.

The dynamic of the history of salvation is also present in the icon since we see how God sends his only Son to sacrifice himself for us and gives us new life through the Spirit. It is captured in the place given to the cup at the center of the icon to which the hands of the Father, Son, and Spirit point. The blessing gesture of the Father empowers and encourages the Son to accept his mission to become the sacrificial lamb, while the Spirit points to the altar where we have access to the sacrifice of the Son for the salvation of the world by sharing in the cup of crucified, self-giving love. But all this is so that we will be drawn into the divine circle of love, life, and tenderness where our true home is and where our ultimate destiny lies.

After the celebration of the eucharist a lady approached me. I knew that she had been with us for some time to care for her dying mother. She informed me that her mother's death was imminent and she made a request that both astonished and exhilarated me: "I would appreciate having Rublev's icon at the front of the church during the funeral liturgy for my mother."

Note

1. Henri J.M. Nouwen, *Behold the Beauty of the Lord: Praying with Icons* (Notre Dame: Ave Maria Press, 1987) 19-27.